design |dəˈzīn|

noun

• a plan or drawing produced to show the look and function or workings of a building, garment, or other object before it is built or made: *she has just unveiled her design for the new museum.*

• the purpose, planning, or intention that exists or is thought to exist behind an action, fact, or material object: *the appearance of design in the universe.*

verb

• to decide upon the look and functioning of (a building, garment, or other object), typically by making a detailed drawing of it: *a number of architectural students were designing a factory.*

Oxford English Dictionary, 3rd Ed.

IN THIS ISSUE

T. A. EDISON.
Electric-Lamp.

No. 223,898.   Patented Jan. 27, 1880.

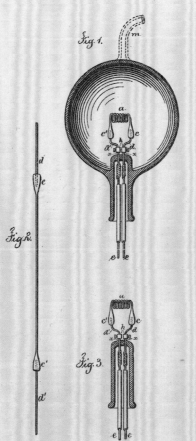

Fig. 1.

Fig. 2.

Fig. 3.

Witnesses

Chas. H. Smith
Geo. T. Pinckney

Inventor

Thomas A. Edison

per Lemuel W. Serrell
atty

LA+ DESIGN
EDITORIAL

According to engineer and physicist Adrian Bejan, featured in this issue, everything designs itself. In his quest for design's unifying theory Bejan posits that all things—natural or artificial—take shape to maximize efficiency for that which flows through them: vascular systems, rivers, cities, airports. But while we share the rudiments of design acumen with many species and processes, its only humans that have designs on the future. And who better to consider the future of design than Winy Maas. In this issue, Javier Arpa interviews Maas on his latest thinking about design's capacity to make the world a better place and how this translates into design education.

In theory, we use design to improve the world, but in practice design can have the opposite effect. Sometimes it does both. Think of the combustion engine liberating us from toil only to give us climate change, or the production of fertilizers to grow cheap food only to pollute our rivers. Think of the absurdity of bottled water using more water in its production than it ultimately contains. Think of all of design's detritus piling up in mega-landfills, which then themselves require design! In their A–Z of design ecology, Craig Bremner and Paul Rodgers sort through the trash and try to make sense of some of design's many broken promises.

Whether we valorize it as the democratization of design or critique it as the perversion of the commodity fetish, designed things are now ubiquitous. Not only things, but entire systems must now be designed and objects reconceived and redesigned as mere moments in unfathomably complex ecological flows. Architects Lizzie Yarina + Claudia Bode explore this different and emerging conception of the object as part of systemic, relational assemblages. The discourse of the Anthropocene now frames the planet itself and even space beyond as a design problem. Looking through the metaphor of the terrarium darkly, Richard Weller revisits classic design failures such as Biosphere II and EPCOT arguing that at the heart of our tinkering with the world is a desire for total environmental control.

Environmental control is essentially now the domain of the digital. Design decisions are increasingly being made based on the available data, but what is often forgotten is that the data is never neutral. As such, designers not only need to become self-conscious about the ways in which data (mis)represents the world, but also actively and creatively engage in making their own data. Architect David Salomon opens up this issue and explores various methods of using data as both fact and fiction in relation to a selection of contemporary projects.

Design impacts lives and manifests certain world views. Design can serve the status quo or destabilize it. In short, design is political. In this regard, Colin Curley interviews Andrés Jaque (Office for Political Innovation) who discusses the role of technology and agency of architecture in society today, and Christopher Marcinkoski interviews Anthony Dunne + Fiona Raby (Dunne + Raby) to discuss how their practice continuously seeks to redefine the role of design in society. The temple where such roles are showcased is the Museum of Modern Art in New York City, and for this issue Daniel Pittman interviews MoMA's senior curator of architecture and design, Paola Antonelli, about new frontiers in the world of design.

Design is political, but it can also be fun and so we leave the museum to meet game designer Colleen Macklin who writes scripts for participatory games in New York's public spaces. Macklin redefines and subverts public space through the agency of play. This playful psychogeography of the city is extended into the textuality of Los Angeles by anthropologist Keith Murphy who shows how different groups of people interact with and give meaning to the landscapes they inhabit. Design is also a question of desire, so moving further into the mind, experimental psychologist Thomas Jacobsen describes how current neurological research is coming closer to understanding the subjectivity of what individuals and cultures consider to be beautiful.

Finally, turning the microscope onto the profession of landscape architecture, James Corner discusses landscape architecture in relation to design culture, Jenni Zell explores life as a woman landscape architect through a Kafkaesque lens, while Thomas Oles challenges stereotypes of landscape architecture's professional identity. And if design still seems like something only related to the aesthetic engines of New York, London, and Milan, we are pleased to publish Dane Carlson's early work as he builds a different design career in the developing world.

In the call for papers for this issue we asked, what does landscape architecture bring to the broader culture of design? What lessons can be learned from other disciplines at the cutting edge of design? What role does design play in a time of transformative technological change? Here, then, are the answers, + some!

Tatum L. Hands + Richard Weller
Issue Editors

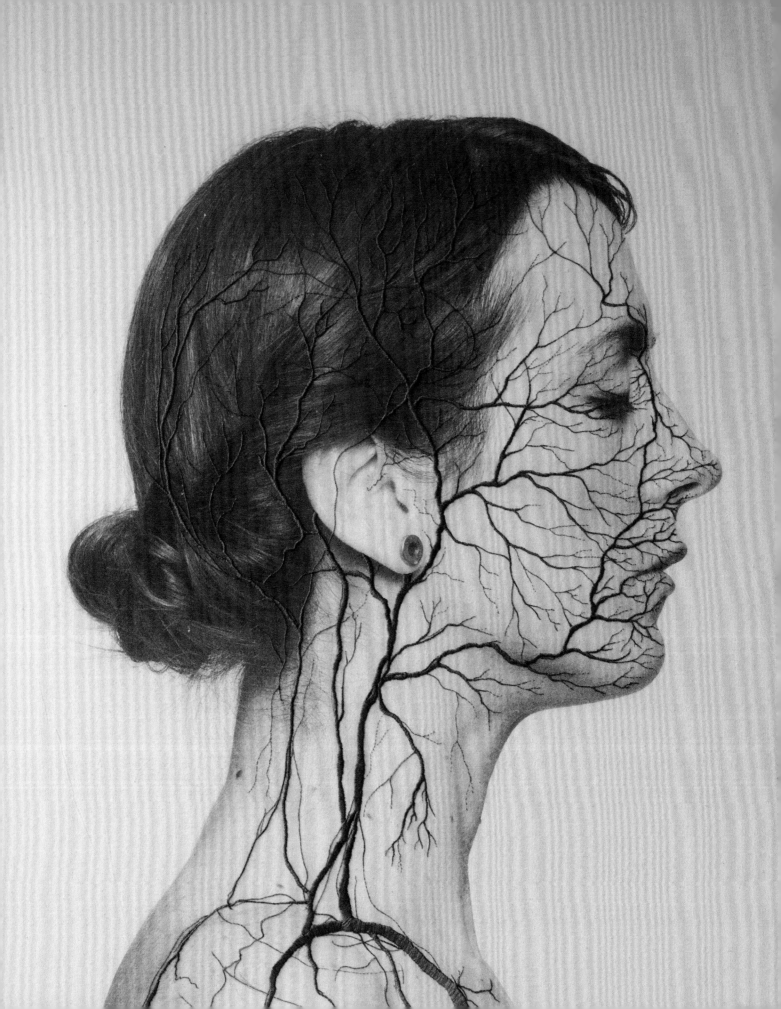

ADRIAN BEJAN

THE EVOLVING DESIGN OF OUR LIFE

Adrian Bejan is the J.A. Jones Distinguished Professor of Mechanical Engineering at Duke University. He holds a PhD from MIT, and has received 18 honorary doctorates from universities in 11 countries. Bejan is the recipient of numerous awards including the 2018 Benjamin Franklin Medal awarded for his "constructal theory, which predicts natural design and its evolution in engineering, scientific, and social systems." He is the author of 30 books, including *Design in Nature* (2012) and *The Physics of Everything* (2016).

✛ PHYSICS, EVOLUTIONARY BIOLOGY, DESIGN

Opposite: "Head" by Juana Gomez, from the *Constructal* series. Hand embroidery and photography on cotton (90x80 cm).

Why do human settlements happen? Why does "social organization" evolve and become more complex as the movement of the members of society increase? Why does the organization become more hierarchical, with striking inequality? The best answer to these questions is a single answer, and the best single answer is the shortest: that's nature.

We are as natural as everything else that moves on earth. We are not only related to the apes, we sweep and renew the earth's surface like the rivers, the rain, and the winds. Conga lines snaking through the impenetrable jungle are prefigurations of social organization. We move on earth with evolving design, and the design morphs while we move. Cities metamorphose by becoming living tissues on a grand scale. We move through the city in overlapping tree-like patterns, like red blood cells in the circulatory system. Air traffic over a continent evolves into arborescent flow structures that morph endlessly, just like river basins, lightning, animal migration routes, and living vascular tissues.

Here, I introduce the reader to constructal law, the physics principle that underpins all evolution, animate and inanimate. Slightly edited, the constructal law reads: for a flow system to persist in time—to live—it must evolve freely to provide easier access to the currents that flow through it.[1] Life is movement, and nature is movement with evolving configuration, or evolutionary design. Compared with this, death is the state where nothing moves and nothing changes. The tree-shaped flows of human presence on earth illustrate how the principle can be used to predict, or to speculate on, the evolution of human life. The principle empowers us to construct and predict our future by configuring our paths and rhythms in ways that facilitate our movement and make human life easier. It's all about flow access. The constructal law accounts

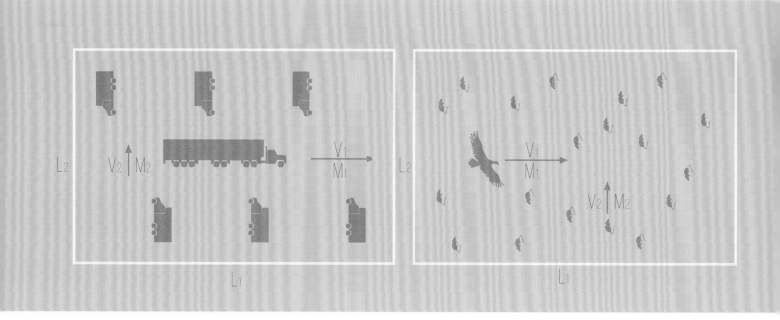

Above: Easiest access to movement on an area is assured by a combination of two kinds of movement: long and fast (depicted on the horizontal plane) and short and slow (depicted on the vertical plane).

for the universal tendency to seek an easier entry to a space (area, volume) and an easier exit. The word "easier" accounts for many common features and descriptions, such as faster, cheaper, more efficient, more economical, and so on.

The drawing—the configuration—that unites all these animate and inanimate flow phenomena is the tree. Not one still image, but sequences of images of tree-shaped flows that evolve in a particular (discernible) direction in time. The design of life on the landscape is like a movie, animated drawings, or cartoons. The flowing design that changes freely (as if with objective) is the universal phenomenon that today is called evolution. To illustrate the physics principle and its predictive value to us, I present some of the most common natural designs of human life and movement.

The City

All roads lead to Rome. This is how the population moving from the countryside (the area) was connected to Rome (the point). Not a radial pattern with roads in all directions, but a tree-shaped one with only a few major arteries leading to the city. This natural design connects every large and small city to its allocated area. The same design connects every river basin and delta to their points of discharge and supply.[2] Streets, highways, and air routes "happen" naturally because

of the phenomenon of economies of scale. It is easier—that is, more efficient—to move through the environment by joining other movers, as opposed to moving alone as one against the environment. This universal tendency is captured by the saying "If you can't beat them, join them."

Movement on the landscape appears complicated because it leaves marks or paths that crisscross and form grids. This is particularly evident in the evolving designs of urban traffic. Less evident is the actual flow of people and goods in an area. Every flow is tree-shaped, from the starting area to the point (or points) of interest. The city grid is the solid, but not permanent, infrastructure that accommodates all the possible tree-shaped flows. The superposition of the big branches of the trees forms the grid of avenues and highways. The superposition of the tree canopies becomes the grid of streets, alleys, lawns, and house floors. This "few large and many small" characteristic of urban design has its origin in the natural design of all tree-shaped flows.

Most people think that the city is the solid infrastructure that we see and draw, houses and streets. No. The city is the human life that flows, morphs, shapes, and reshapes the surface called city. The solid infrastructure morphs along with the flows that it facilitates. The solid infrastructure is

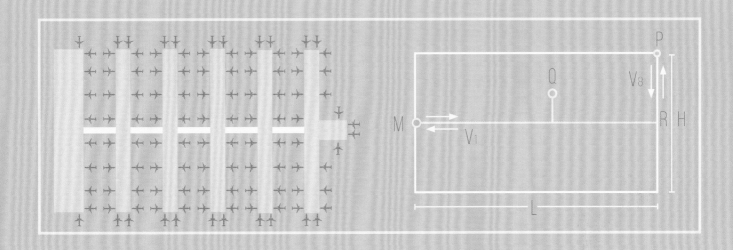

Above: The Atlanta airport design serves as an example of all the imaginable flows that happen naturally to connect points with areas and volumes.

not permanent; it is like a movie. The solid skeleton of the animal evolves along with all the flows that it supports, which constitute the evolving and surviving animal. To reduce the description of the living system to its solid infrastructure misses the physics of life.

Two Ways to Flow are Better than One

Few large and many small is the hierarchy in the movement of freight on the globe. The movement is facilitated when a special balance is established between the number of small vehicles allocated to (and moving the same freight as) one large vehicle, and when an additional balance (the area shape L_1/L_2) is established between the distances (L_1, L_2) traveled by the few and the many. Few large and many small is also how animal mass moves, whether by land, water, or air. The design of animal mass movement is the precursor to our own design as the "human and machine species" sweeping and reshaping the earth's surface.[3]

A large airport without trains, or without walking, cannot compete on the same area with the design that combines walking with riding on a vehicle. The Atlanta airport is an excellent illustration of the seed from which all forms of urban and natural flow networks have grown. On a fixed area ($A = HL$) with variable shape (the ratio H/L) and two speeds (walking,

V_0, and riding on a train, V_1), the time of travel from P to M (or from all points Q to M, averaged over A) is minimum when the shape is $H/L = 2V_0/V_1$. The walking time (PR) is equal to the riding time (RM). The long and fast travel is balanced with the short and slow travel.

The movement of everything (people, freight, vehicles) happens because it reaches a balance, a trade-off, between two very different kinds of movement: short and slow (walking), and long and fast (riding a vehicle). When the balance is reached, the flow configuration is born on the world map: the paths through a forest, a city, the air traffic system. The resulting design is the "tree" movie of human life on earth. It is no different than the life of any river. The time needed by rain water to seep down the hill slope to the river is the same as the time spent by the same water as a river, from the hill slope to the sea. With this principle it is easy to see in retrospect the birth and evolution of the most familiar examples of human design on earth: the harbor, the city, the city block, the airport, the city grid, the dry-stone constructions of antiquity (the Pyramids), and the most modern features of urban design (beltways, tunnels, overpasses).

In a thriving economy, a city grows in size while the speed of travel on the streets lags behind the speed available on

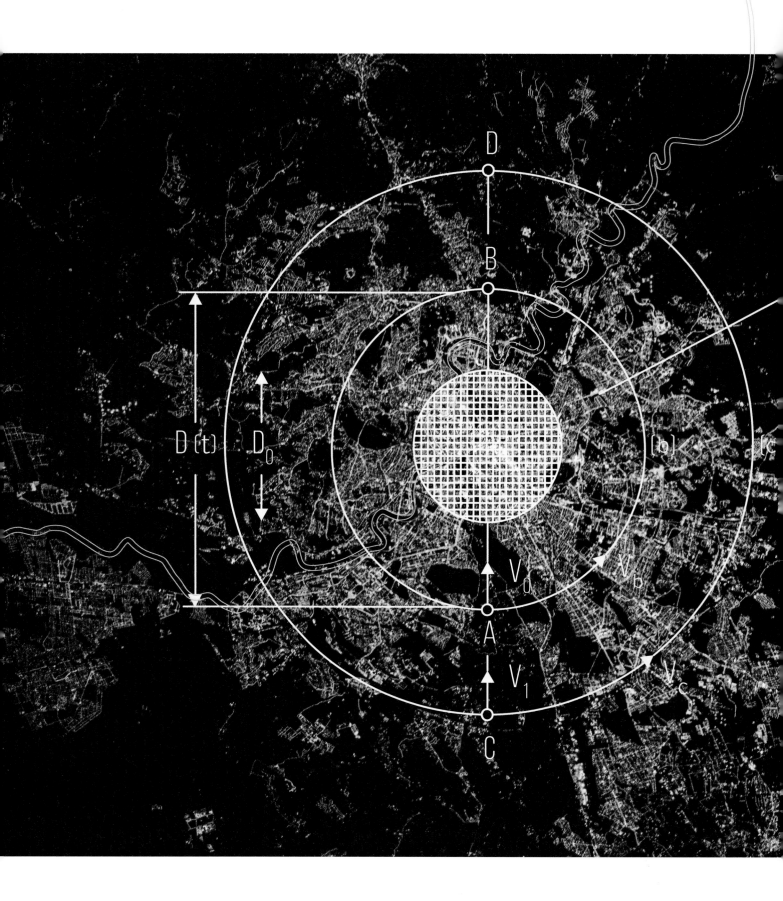

[time]

highways, which increases in time. When the city size becomes large enough, the access between two diametrically opposed points on the city perimeter is made easier (faster) by a beltway. As the city size and highway speed continue to increase, a new beltway, larger than the first, offers even greater access than the first beltway. Although the growth (size, speed) is gradual, the morphology of vascular flow on the area changes stepwise, dramatically. Such is life and evolution: gradual and stepwise, birth and extinction, all hand in glove, in harmony. The city phenomenon shows how that evolution is predictable.[4]

Pedestrian Flow

The balancing of times and the search for greater flow access for everybody are mental viewings that take the thinker well beyond the trees overlapping on areas of cities and river basins. The same idea works in three dimensions. A tall building works well when its elevators are fast enough so that the time spent on the vertical is comparable with the time walking horizontally along corridors. Security checkpoints in airports and war zones work best when the time and effort spent in the bottlenecks are comparable to that spent en route to them. The infrastructure and security of a previously virgin or newly liberated area owe their designs to the same principle as all other design phenomena.

Branching walkways are the simplest trees. When their space (floor area) is constrained, the fastest pedestrian flow is when the trunk is wider than the branch, such that their widths form a special ratio. Aisles (whether for arenas or airplanes) should be tapered, such that the aisle width is greater where the pedestrian flow rate is greater. Easiest access into and out of a tall building can be achieved by shaping the building such that there is a special balance between the size of the floor area and the height of the elevator shaft.

Fuel and Wealth

Nothing moves unless it is driven by power. The power comes from engines of all kinds and sizes, and engines consume fuel. The earth engine is fueled by heat from the sun, and drives all movement on earth – the winds, the oceanic currents, the circuit executed by water (rain, rivers, evaporation), and all the animal movement including ours. The fuel for animals is food, which comes from the growth (vegetation, animal) driven by solar heating and the ensuing water flow. The fuel for humans is of many kinds: food, fossil, and renewable, directly from the sun.

In this article we see that the human movement is distributed hierarchically on earth. Natural hierarchy manifests itself in the few large and many small, and the time balance between short (slow) travel and long (fast) travel. The point is that because the human movement on earth is hierarchical, so is the consumption of fuel. The graphs on the following page showing 2006 data from the International Energy Agency confirm this. Look on the abscissa: the annual world consumption of fuel is distributed "unequally" on the globe.

This feature is evident no matter how you look at the data: country by country, or per capita. The message of these graphs is on the ordinate. Annual wealth (GDP) is proportional to annual fuel consumption, and it is distributed just as unequally. Said another way, wealth inequality (hierarchy) emerges naturally because it is a record (a measurement, in economics) of the hierarchical flow of people and vehicles that consume fuel hierarchically, because their movement sweeps the globe with hierarchy, not uniformity. Wealth inequality is difficult to erase because the hierarchical character of all movement emerges naturally out of the human tendency toward what's easier.

The Future

The evolution of human settlements happens naturally because it is governed by its law of physics. The Occupy Movement, which saw protesters seize public squares, was intended to highlight wealth inequality and lack of freedom. But it provided an unintended lesson on the design of cities: access is the future of urban design.

That was evident to observers who compared Occupy Wall Street in New York and Occupy Central in Hong Kong. The squatters in New York brought a wide section of the city around its Financial District to a standstill in 2011, and that gridlock produced strong resentment from residents and businesses. The reason for the standstill was the interrupted flow of pedestrian and auto traffic in downtown New York, which is mainly on a horizontal plane at street level. For all its skyscrapers and subways, much of New York is two-dimensional.

Hong Kong is different. At the height of the Occupy Central movement, the protesters squatting there did not stop the pedestrian and auto traffic because that city's central business district is 'vascularized' in three dimensions, with overpasses, underpasses, and loops for pedestrians and vehicles. Compared to New York, access for inhabitants and businesses in Hong Kong was not impaired. While the protesters were forced out of New York after eight weeks, Occupy Central was tolerated for 10 months. Access of an even more basic kind is why the Occupy movement in Hong Kong lasted much longer than in New York. The urge to have freedom is more unifying than the urge to reduce wealth inequality.

Human settlements will continue to emerge hierarchically. On any finite territory the population will live in one big city, two or three smaller cities, and so on, all the way to numerous tiny settlements (villages) on the land. All in harmony, all thriving, all needing each other. Large hubs and major channels—for example, air routes and commercial aircraft—will always flow together with smaller hubs and numerous smaller channels. Flowing through the large and the small is the same population, you and I. The fine channels will continue to be allocated to area interstices that are covered by ground movement—people, and all the animate and the inanimate flows of the environment. The time to travel long and fast

(along channels) will continue to be comparable with the time to travel short and slow (across the areas between channels). Nobody will hurry up to wait.

The designs of the Atlanta airport, Rhodes, and Rome were not copied from nature. Their emergence and persistence as living flow systems are nature itself. Now we know the principle that underlies their evolution, scaling rules, and longevity. Every flow is from a point to an infinite number of points (area or volume), and from an infinite number of points to one point. This is why the flow architectures of nature and society evolve as overlapping tree-shaped hierarchies. Had nature been one-dimensional, on an axis, not in space, all the flows would have been point-to-point, and their paths would have been straight segments, ugly and uninteresting.

Thus we render biomimetics obsolete because the constructal law allows us to predict and explain the designs that emerge and evolve naturally. Copying the drawings from a handbook is the most common approach, and it leads to marching in place, not to leaping forward. Copying an inventor's revolutionary design is much more effective, but such leaps are either costly or illegal. With the constructal law we are the inventors, the far-seers.

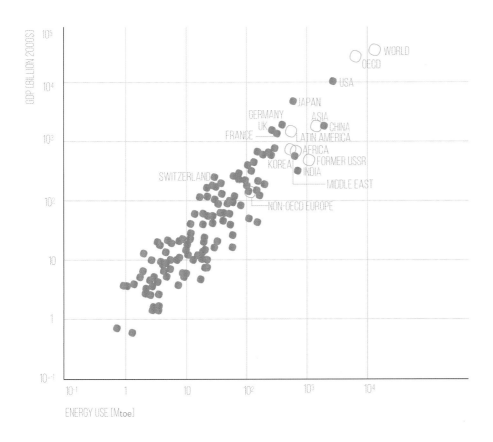

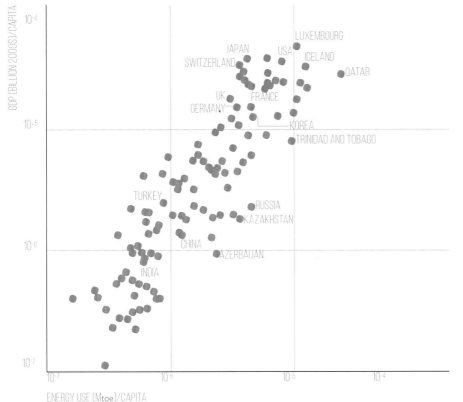

1 Adrian Bejan & J. Peder Zane, *Design in Nature: How the Constructal Law Governs Evolution in Biology, Physics, Technology, and Social Organization* [New York: Doubleday, 2012]: Adrian Bejan, The Physics of Life: The Evolution of Everything [New York: St. Martin's Press, 2016].

2 When I discovered the constructal law in September 1995, I faced a dilemma: in which language should I express this idea first? Should it be fluid mechanics and hydrology, as in the birth of tree-shaped hierarchy in a river basin? Should it be heat transfer, as in the tree-shaped conducting paths for heat evacuation from a box filled with electronics? Instead, I chose the language that we all know and speak—the city—which is the icon of civilization. My first constructal-law paper [June 1996] was titled "Street Network Theory of Organization in Nature." The fluid mechanics and heat transfer formulations of the same mental viewing came soon after.

3 Bejan & Zane, *Design in Nature,* ibid; Bejan, *The Physics of Life*, ibid.

4 Ibid.

Previous: As a city's population and territory grows, travel across the city through the grid becomes "slow" in comparison with the alternative provided by a beltway around the city grid.

Left: As shown in these graphs, the natural hierarchy found in human movement is reflected in unequal wealth and fuel consumption.

IN CONVERSATION WITH
WINY MAAS

Winy Maas is co-founder of architecture and urban design practice MVRDV, and director of The Why Factory at Delft University of Technology in the Netherlands. At the turn of the millennium, MVRDV burst onto the global scene with the publication of *Metacity/Datatown* – a set of what would become known as "datascapes" resulting from a straightforward question: how to stuff 260 million Europeans and everything they need to survive into a 400 km x 400 km landscape? Following the question to its logical conclusions not only exposed the contradictions in the pious idealism of sustainability, it compressed architecture and landscape together into a vision of urbanism that was at once alarming and compelling. In succeeding years through their provocative built works and theoretical propositions, MVRDV and The Why Factory have relentlessly explored and amplified the potential of design to engage with issues of high-density living in an age of ecological limits, economic constraints, and democratic design delivery. Fearless, clear eyed, and yet somehow also fun, Winy Maas is about as close as anyone has come to being genuinely visionary in the 21st century without a shred of romanticism. For this dedicated *LA+ DESIGN* issue, **Javier Arpa** sat down with Maas to explore his thoughts on the future of design and design education.

+ As the Earth enters the Anthropocene, design is confronted not just with the design of a site, but with the design of the planet as a whole. At Delft University of Technology, where you lead the think tank The Why Factory, you are currently conducting the research "Planet Maker," which is based on formulating hypothetical future scenarios for the entire planet. Why this research project now?

Well, this research is now more necessary than ever. Besides climate change, we live in a context of generalized fear against globalization and data control, of growing nationalism in Europe or skepticism about the growth of China that touches us all. "Planet Maker" is an attempt to put the global agenda again on the forefront. It explores myriad issues (from the smallest to the largest scale), and tries to reveal how the planet will change spatially in technical, social, or economical terms when looking at one variable at a time, and how we can participate more actively in that as architects and planners.

+ What is the methodology applied in the "Planet Maker" research?

The future of planet Earth is explored through multiple "what ifs" organized through six key lenses: economy, food, energy, mobility, green, and society. Each lens explores scenario-making what ifs and their variants in time through a simulation game that uses scripting tools to manage massive quantities of data and parameters. Can we make planets that are truly green? Can we make a planet that can cool down instead of heating up? That can be open and free? That reduces poverty?

For every lens, students have developed a specific method to tackle correlations between the most pressing subjects, yet all lenses are tested through a common database and a common output of land use. Starting by giving an overview of the most challenging futures, the lenses then go on to explore the what ifs simulating the effects of precise spatial policies. This mini software informs and guides the creation of 48 heat-map globes that test the what ifs of the emerging Anthropocene.

+ So, in this way, will the world become a design product?

Yes, indeed, more than ever. But understanding the world as a design product is not new. The CIAM did it already in the first half of the 20th century. Some totalitarian regimes tried to do it, too; so one could say there is a certain danger in trying to design the planet. But there are lots of thinkers who have also explored it. Paul Virilio, for instance, looked at the planet as a product, as an object to work upon. More recently, design shows such as the Dutch Design Week in Eindhoven are full of products to make the world. There is an incurable desire—despite the localness of certain politicians—to understand the world that we live and work in, and trying to escape this trend is impossible.

+ Are these scenarios or these products reliant on technological progress only?

No, definitely not. Even though I love technology and teach at a technical university, issues such as behaviorism or economics have a profound influence on the scenarios or products that we elaborate. As technicians, we can probably solve scenarios involving flying cars or green roofs more easily, but we cannot forget economy, society, or politics. What does a world without borders look like? What if wealth is evenly distributed and there is only middle class around the globe? We cannot forget those issues; we need to look at the evolution of the planet through all sorts of lenses.

+ As you reminded us in your statement as Ambassador of the Dutch Design Week 2017, "we live in a world experiencing dramatic climate change, declining resources, huge differences in income, extensive political/social disagreement, rapid population growth, substantial consumption of food, water, energy, oxygen, and threats of populism, nationalism, and globalization." In this context, how do design disciplines need to work to provide solutions?

When there is a threat, an agenda is needed in order to beat that threat. And this agenda needs to cover from the very small scale to the very large. Design disciplines need to provide a range of products that fulfill this agenda. These products range from chairs to computers to cars. In other words, all consumer goods—everything, including clothing, construction products, or wine—are part of the Anthropocene era we are in, and we need to act on each of them to mitigate the threats. So, the agenda of design has to cover every product, not less. After all, everything is urbanism!

+ What is the future city that these products will create?

There is not one single future city. The future city needs to adapt to different climates and economies, it needs to adapt itself to time. The future city is open to many interpretations, so the best way to describe it is as a sequence of desires or necessities, which are very wide. This width triggers diversity, flexibility, and mostly freedom. I believe the beauty of the future city lies in that [cultivated] freedom.

+ Your recent involvement in the Dutch Design Week and your continued work for the Dutch Design Foundation have let you know first-hand the state of current Dutch design. How have design professions [landscape, planning, architecture, engineering, urbanism, etc.] evolved in the last 25 years in the Netherlands?

As *SuperDutch*[1] indicated, there was some kind of dictatorship of design coming from the Netherlands in the '80s. It comprised all scales, from object design to landscape architecture. It was a very top-down manifestation–yet still a collective enterprise–which, thanks to the potential of Dutch artificiality, was capable of producing beautiful landscapes that did not exist in other places.

But things have changed in the last 10 years. There is a lot more design coming from other countries, and a small country like the Netherlands is forced to work on experimentation more than ever before so as to overcome competition. What I find special about the current state of Dutch design is precisely its continuous love for experimentation and inventing. If you compare the Dutch Design Week with the *Salone del Mobile di Milano*, the Dutch edition really feels like MIT's Media Lab in relation to Milan's commercial atmosphere and focus.

The state of current Dutch design is the result of a social context in which the creative class is maybe dominated by "hipsters"–the so-called "beard freaks"–more than ever before. I mean, by individuals that work by themselves. There are fewer and fewer corporate firms [MVRDV is maybe the last corporate firm somehow] because all of us are one-person companies, individuals working with their laptops at the corner of a street. The Dutch design environment is dominated by "jet-set beards" capable of lifting design experimentation to incredibly high levels.

+ Do you think the world still watches Dutch design with the same degree of amazement as in the 1990s?

I do think that's still the case. There is an art of designing based on that Golden Age we spoke about earlier that is probably inaugurating a second Golden Age of Dutch Design. If you go to Rotterdam or Eindhoven, you see an incredibly good and productive contribution to the advancement of design at all scales.

+ So, is there still a lot for the world to learn from Dutch design?

Yes, there is. Dutch Design is still empowered by the country's smallness and a sort of vulnerability that triggers both talent and a capacity to trade that serve as fruitful motors for creation.

+ The design process of MVRDV is driven by a mixture of quantitative and qualitative research. Central to this approach is a strong belief that architecture and urbanism are "devices" that can shape and improve our environment in ways that are often quantifiable. The human-made landscape is one that consists of data–in other words, a datascape–which can be visually presented as the quantifiable forces that influence and define the work of architects and urban designers. Datascapes were presented first in *FARMAX* [1998] and further developed in *KM3* [2005]. To what extent are datascapes a technique or a tool in the work of MVRDV nowadays?

The first thing to say is that, even more than we knew in 1998, the world is governed by data. We need more statistical data than ever before. This is a reality that has overcome the instinct or intuition I had 20 years ago when we worked with very basic computers. We need to understand current data flows and trends so as to understand the technology or economics of a project. We all expect answers, we want to find new markets in order to survive, or to convince, or to become independent from certain things. The diagraming which came out of the datascapes still helps a lot to show the end of certain logics.

Currently, we are making an analysis of the skyscrapers of Shenzhen, where over 5,000+ 150m-tall towers are being built. They are all extruded elements with one small "tweak" that differentiates one from the other. They form a collection that can be visited there. After analyzing so many tweaks you realize there is a limit to the technique of tweaking that you, as a designer, can apply. You realize it is necessary to innovate, to go beyond the technique of tweaking and introduce new typologies. That is also a datascape and we are applying it now.

+ You founded The Why Factory 10 years ago, and have taught in numerous design schools throughout the world. Over this decade, do you think educational institutions have undergone a process of homogenization?

In a way, yes, they have. Many schools copy whatever is successful at other institutions. Why? Because students want that. And more and more educational institutions simply consider students as customers. Both the homogenization of education caused by client-oriented thinking and the generalized copycat formula are very dangerous tendencies.

With The Why Factory I initially tried to do something unique in one place: to think about the future city. Ten years later you can see that every school also has some kind of group thinking about the future city. When it comes to robotization, for instance, MIT's Media Lab did a very good job. And now, everybody is trying to do the same.

Due to the homogenization of the last 10 years, universities and academic institutions are all competing. They kill themselves for funds, pushed by certain politicians who, thinking of education in pure market terms, say it's very good for universities to compete. However, this is a quite dangerous trend that may damage research, and the depth and acceleration of knowledge, as certain research lines require concentration and massive amounts of funds to invest in machinery and make tests. The fragmentation resulting from the homogenization of education and research goes against the accumulation necessary to undertake certain kinds of sophisticated work. Super stupid.

+ The School of Design at TU Delft, like many other schools, is divided (and subdivided) into various disciplinary compartments. Is this a good thing?

No, not necessarily. Delft is subdivided into the departments of building technology, architecture, urbanism, etc., which need to fulfill very general educational goals to more students than ever [before]. This results in a lack of culture of collaboration and innovation or depth in the research. The fragmentation into departments is definitely not a good model for research.

Having said that, I'm aware that certain subjects need some concentration and a large specialized team to make things happen. It'll be much more interesting in the future to create one group that does everything on wood technology for the whole planet, or one that specializes on robots. As I said earlier, concentration is often essential.

+ At the beginning of the design studios at The Why Factory students are told that they will be confronted with a very different way of learning. What makes The Why Factory different from other design schools?

At The Why Factory we work with the future city in abstract terms. That's not done in many places. Our projects are site-less. We paint the future city in an abstract way, so that our visions can be applied everywhere. I think that this is rare because most design studios in master's [level] education are, I would say, too site specific. This method challenges students because they have to think in abstract terms.

The success of The Why Factory is in part due to the liberty resulting from this abstraction. It creates a kind of area of freedom for students that can later be applied upon their return to China or Russia. Students don't leave The Why Factory with a design for Trafalgar Square in their portfolios. Who cares about that? The kind of more generic knowledge we provide allows students to act as global citizens and find a career everywhere. I think that's the advantage of abstraction. The second element is that we do a comparative research, undertaken by students collectively. There is no individual work, but a comparative approach that makes projects stronger and deeper. And for students, it clarifies their position in relation to others.

+ The Why Factory has worked for a decade on the agenda of the future of our cities. Yet the outcome, design research, is commonly regarded as an "unscientific" method. Why do you think that is?

At least in master's education you can never become hyper-scientific, as you simply do not have the time for doing it. What we do is speculative. It is research and research-driven, but it cannot be considered scientific research. It's research in the sense that it wants to explore data or topics that are happening on the planet.

+ The outcome of The Why Factory's work is what you call "visionary." Can you define more precisely what being visionary means to you?

Being visionary is working on making the future less unknown. The visionary tries to convince others that there is a direction possible for the planet. I train students to think in that way, and hope to educate future leaders in architecture and urbanism. There are schools that teach leadership in many other fields, but not in the fields of architecture and urbanism. Schools of architecture should teach leadership, but I don't see it. The London School of Economics and the Erasmus University are doing that within the fields of economics and politics. Why not us within urbanism and architecture?

+ How does the speculative work undertaken by The Why Factory translate into the practice of MVRDV? How do knowledge, research, or design circulate between The Why Factory and MVRDV?

I try to disconnect The Why Factory from MVRDV, but that's very hard, of course. We don't use our students to design office spaces for us so as to test office concepts that you could apply in China. That's not happening. But what we do at The Why Factory certainly leads to inspiration. That's very true. We researched the "Vertical Village," which has deeply influenced MVRDV's work. More recently the "Wego House," an investigation undertaken by The Why Factory, counted on MVRDV to materialize it into a 1:1 model presented during a past edition of the Dutch Design Week in Eindhoven. I do believe that there are certain points of contact between academia and the commercial world, but there is still an independency to be kept between one and the other.

+ When you lecture around the world, you use the phrase "what's next?" repeatedly in less than one hour, keeping a tension among the audience who wait impatiently for the next discovery to be revealed. What's next in The Why Factory's agenda?

That's a very good question: what to do after 10 years of research? In the first place, since things are slow, and despite our eagerness to accelerate, we still need to publish several books we have in the pipeline. I do think that our method is far from dead yet, that the subjects we are embracing are not dead yet, and that there are still a lot of things to do. In the meantime, certain topics need updates, like the "Green Dream." Also, the "Space-Fighter," a software that brings together all parametric knowledge on spatial design, is not there yet.

+ How do you see The Why Factory in 10 years from now?

Oh, I don't know. That's a hard question. I would love to work with more universities on the planet in the next 10 years. I would like to find more funds to deepen our investigation and to get more things done. I admire Norman Foster for being able to setup his Foundation in Madrid. He found sufficient sponsors to make such an enterprise happen. It's fantastic. I wouldn't mind following such a path.

+ Since the 1990s, "landscape urbanism theory argued that rather than coming in at the end of a design and planning process, landscape architects should be leading the large interdisciplinary teams that were becoming standard for large urban development projects." "The crux of the landscape urbanism approach rests on the appreciation of the underlying landscape systems of any given site [geological, hydrological, ecological, and social] as drivers of urbanization." Do you agree with this vision?

Let's take the term landscape architecture one step further. If we make cities in the future that are made of self-growing biological material that reacts to your input, then we have the ultimate, say, landscape city. In that moment, the landscape architect ceases to exist and is replaced by biologists: crypto-biologists. I find that a good statement: landscape architects will become crypto-biologists. Therefore, if crypto-biology can take over, crypto-biologists will be the new politicians.

1 Bart Lootsma, *SuperDutch: New Architecture in the Netherlands* [Princeton Architectural Press, 2000].

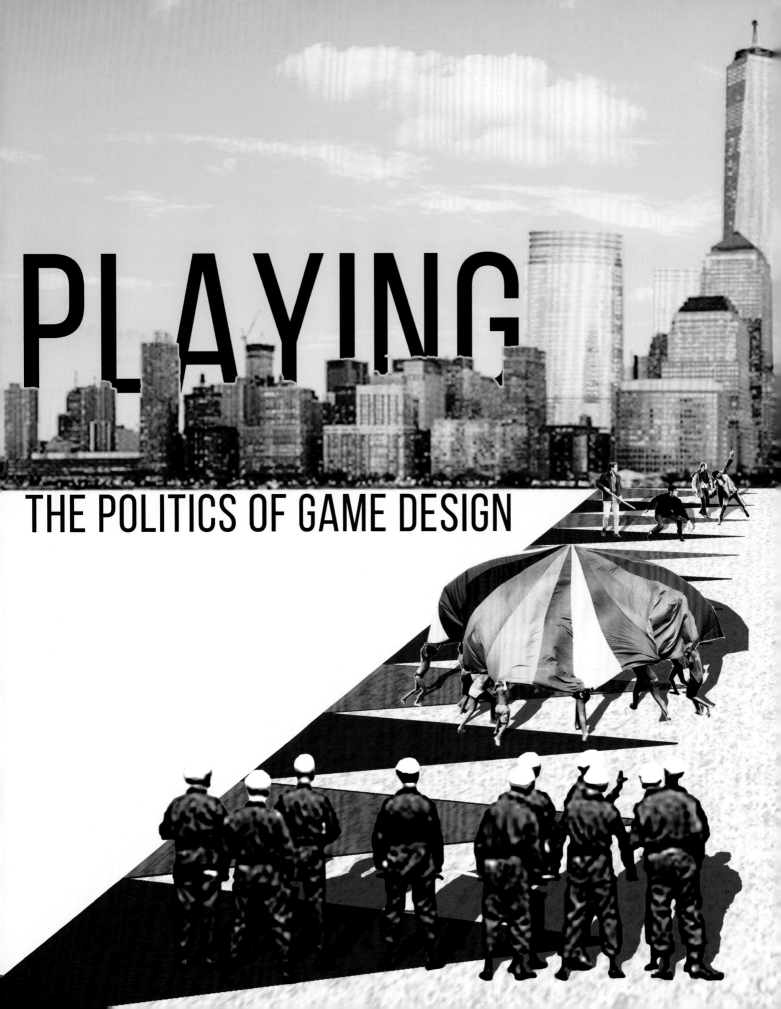

PLAYING

THE POLITICS OF GAME DESIGN

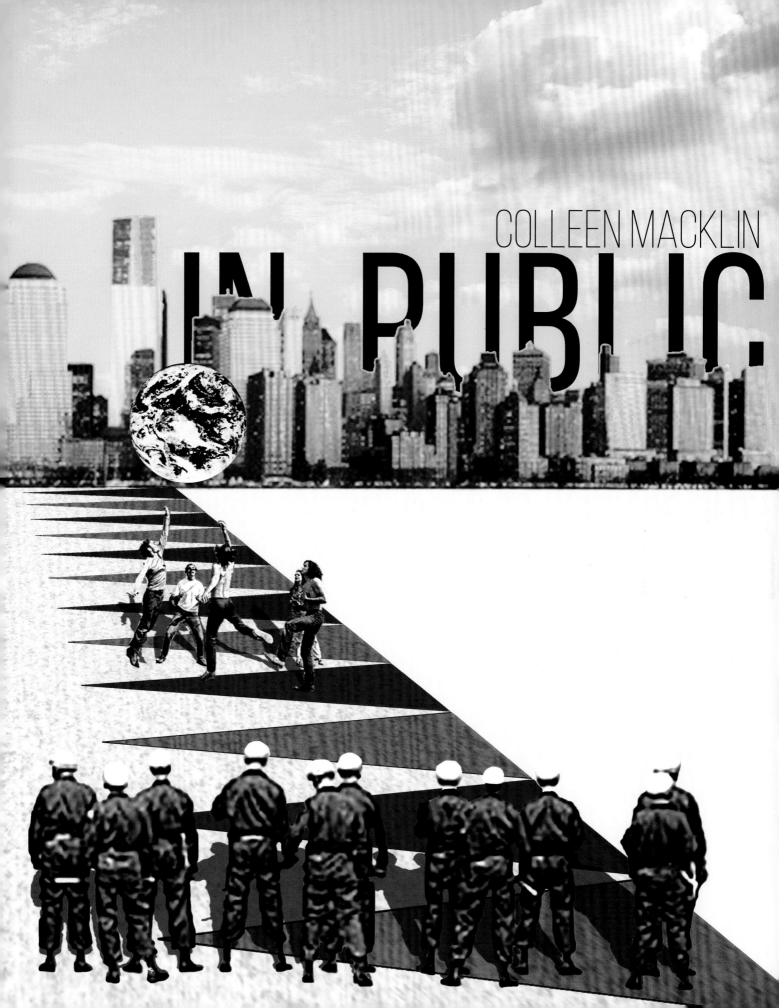

Colleen Macklin is a game designer, professor at Parsons School of Design, and founder and co-director of PETLab (Prototyping Education and Technology Lab), where she develops games for experiential learning and social engagement, including Re:Activism. She is a member of Local No. 12, creators of the card game, The Metagame, and coauthor of *Games, Design and Play: A Detailed Look at Iterative Game Design* (2016). Parachute games were her favorite subject in school.

✦ GAME DESIGN

Do you remember playing with a parachute when you were a kid? For the last few years, I've been performing a little informal survey, asking this question to friends and strangers. The number of people who answer yes, regardless of where they grew up, is surprising. I would make the unscientific pronouncement that it's about 90%. Perhaps, reader, you answered yes to this question too!

If not, I'll describe this playing with parachutes thing briefly. It starts with everyone in a circle, surrounding the outside edge of the parachute facing each other. A facilitator–usually a responsible adult–tells us what to do. We collaborate to lift our edge of the parachute and it rises above our heads like a mushroom cloud. We follow the orders to walk into the center towards each other and sit down, the parachute enclosing us in a tent, it's just us, the world falls away. But eventually the parachute falls too, and we lose sight of each other buried in its soft fabric. This is the tip of the iceberg in parachute play. There's a whole series of parachute drills, "popcorn," "waves," "parachute tag" – each participant pulling in unison to make magic happen. Well, not always in unison. Some choose to defect from the collective and push down while everyone else pulls up, which is fun too – at least for the defectors, as their individual action ripples out to affect the whole. For many, managing these parachute misfits and their own impulses to become one, is as political as parachute play gets; a tiny version of the age-old struggle between the individual and the collective. But did you know that the rise of parachute play began as a political movement and form of protest? This essay links parachute games in playgrounds to protest games in public, each demonstrating that, as the influential game designer Bernie DeKoven claims, "playing in public itself, is a political act."[1]

First, let's travel back in time to Northern California, 1973. There we might witness thousands of pacifists frolicking by the Pacific Ocean, playing with parachutes. And Earth balls. And with each other. Engaging in the kind of close-contact physical horseplay that we would require waivers for these days. They're playing games with goofy names like Ooh Ahh, or Prui, or the more descriptively titled Hug Tag. These were "New Games," guided by the mantra "play hard, play fair, nobody hurt."[2] The event we're witnessing is the first ever New Games Tournament, on the golden hills of the 2,200-acre Gerbode Preserve, a few miles north of the Golden Gate Bridge in San Francisco. The Nature Conservancy decided that this would be the preserve's first public event, a multi-weekend event, "for the community to relate to its natural environment in a new and creative way."[3] Back to this idyllic event in a moment. First, we must answer the question, why is playing with parachutes political?

The New Games movement had its start a few years earlier at a 1966 event for the San Francisco War Resisters League cheekily called "World War IV." It was orchestrated by Stewart Brand, who wasn't yet, but would be known for the *Whole Earth Catalog* (incidentally, he was also a former Army Ranger parachutist). At Brand's event, anti-war activists incongruously engaged in combat, a battle to the "death" wearing socks on wrestling mats, accompanied by a live rock-band soundtrack. They were playing the game Slaughter, a Twister-meets-the-Thunderdome spectacle created by Brand to translate the increasingly cerebral and "heavy" discourse of anti-war activism into something more physical and immediate. As he puts it, "I felt that American combat was being pushed as far away as the planet would allow, becoming abstract and remote. It suggested to me that there was something wrong with our conflict forms here."[4]

Brand wanted to help participants put aside their entrenched positions and understand war by "appreciating and experiencing the source of it within themselves."[5] This was anti-violent violence, play as catharsis, or as Brand called it, "Softwar."[6] The event's finale was a battle for the planet, represented by a six-foot diameter Earthball – a repurposed canvas ball used by Brand in army bootcamp training, but this time painted with swirling clouds, oceans, and jagged continents to resemble a view of our planet from space (prefiguring the famous 1968 cover of the *Whole Earth Catalog*). The singular goal of the game was to get the giant Earthball from one end of the field to the other, teams competing to push the ball to the opposite end of the field. However, to Brand's excitement, when the ball neared one of the goals, players on the winning team quickly joined the losing team to push the ball the other way. They had changed the rules! The game went on for more than an hour without a goal; as Brand remarked, "their unspoken and accepted agreement had been to play, as long and hard as possible."[7]

From this event grew the New Games movement, bringing aggressive and physical play to the peaceniks, while pacifying military technologies like parachutes and bootcamp balls into Softwar sporting goods. This is how playing with a parachute has its roots in protest.

While the anti-war sentiment of playing with a parachute may be unbeknownst to most first-graders, the subversive and transformative aspects of play in public demonstrated by those early days of New Games still hold. A few years ago, New Games facilitator, game designer, and "fun-theorist" Bernie DeKoven, described the lesson learned from New Games: "Playfulness itself, especially when you are playing in public, is a political act. Because you are demonstrating to people the freedom to play."[8] DeKoven, whose book *The Well-Played Game* articulates and expands upon the New Games mindset, believed that playing with others was a practice of what he called "coliberation," a higher form of collaboration where the players' sole purpose was to create and maintain a play community.[9] For Brand, DeKoven, and the other founders of New Games, playing in public equaled a playfully utopian politics. Fred Turner describes this political turn as the culmination of New Game elements and practices:

> The arrangement of players and observers on the field, the construction of rules (or the lack of them), the deployment of technologies and techniques in and around the space defined for play – for the New Gamers, to rearrange these elements was to rearrange the structure of society itself. In that sense, the New Gamers were not only playing but committing politics.[10]

If we were to move our time-travel oculus from 1970s California to the Parisian neighborhood of Saint-Germain-des-Prés just a few years earlier, we might see an interesting application of playful politics by players of a different game: the Dérive.[11] A group calling themselves The Letterists (ur-form of the better-known Situationists) invented the Dérive, a day-long "drift" through the city, dropping all work and leisure to "let themselves be drawn by the attractions of the terrain and the encounters they find there."[12] This pleasure-based pedestrianism finds a home in Situationist Constant Nieuwenhuys's *New Babylon* (originally known as *Dériville*), a city of play built on top of the old capitalist city, transforming daily reality into play for "Homo Ludens" as they seek "to transform, to recreate, those surroundings, that world, according to [their] new needs."[13] A thread of the Situationist's politics was based in public play, to recreate politics through recreation, so to speak – a theme shared by The Situationists and their younger, American New Games cousins. Both were borne of the protests of the 1960s: New Games in reaction to the Vietnam War, the Situationists marked by the 1968 labor protests of Paris. And both were overlaying the rules of the city with their own.

This is what we do when we're playing with parachutes– overlaying the rules defining what parachutes typically do with new rules to transform it into something else–a trampoline for beach balls, a tent, a communal interface. Games do this too – they transform the world into a playspace. A game is made up of a few basic elements: players, the playspace (or field of play), objects (parachutes, for example), goals, actions, and perhaps most importantly, rules to account for them all.[14] While the elements sound simple, designing games is also challenging, because it entails solving second-order design problems. Game Designers Katie Salen and Eric Zimmerman describe this concept well: "As a game designer, you are never directly designing the behavior of your players. Instead, you are only designing the rules of the system."[15] And it's the rules in a game that generate play.

The challenges inherent in not being able to directly design behavior likely resonates with architects and designers of public space. Game design is second order design, as is the design of cities and public spaces. One can establish a space – but it is always, in games and architecture, a space of possibilities. Architectural historian Iain Bordon articulates this point as he explores how skateboarders reimagine urban infrastructure in *Skateboarding, Space and the City*.[16] And architect Raoul Bunschoten leverages the second-order commonality between games and the design of public spaces by designing board games to test public space design.[17]

However, despite the shared design concerns of game designers and spatial designers, the rules the general public encounters in games and in public spaces are perceived quite differently. To most, there's two types of rules. Rules in a game, and rules everywhere else. Rules in a game lead to fun, while the rules one encounters in a park, for instance, are limiting. For example, The National Park Service rules for the former site of the New Games Tournament details how bicycles, picnics, and even games can happen, such as where it's possible to play "small impromptu pickup games that do not adversely impact the designated natural and cultural resources."[18] It would be much more difficult for the New Games Tournament of the 1970s to happen now based on the rules that have evolved in the preserve since its inception in the 1970s.

The rules in games, on the other hand, create space and enable a type of activity that tests the limits of the rules themselves through *play*. As Johan Huizinga, in his canonical *Homo Ludens* describes:

> All play moves and has its being within a playground that is marked off beforehand either materially or ideally, deliberately or as a matter of course...The arena, the card-table, the magic circle, the temple, the stage, the tennis court, the court of justice, etc., all are in form and function play-grounds...within which special rules obtain. All are temporary worlds within the ordinary world, dedicated to the performance of an act apart.[19]

The great paradox of games is that play emerges from a structured set of rules. And when we place liberating game rules on top of the delimiting rules of public space (both legally explicit and socially implicit), we turn that space into a play-ground, "temporary worlds within the ordinary world." And then, interesting things happen.

Re:Activism[20] is a game about activism – in particular, a game tracing the history of protests as players reenact and reinterpret these moments in the locations where they happened. Re:Activism has been played around the nation, on the streets of New York to Minneapolis/St. Paul, to Philadelphia, to Atlanta. It debuted in New York City as part of the 2008 Come Out and Play festival, an annual celebration of street games. One might describe Re:Activism as a "new" New Game; it is philosophically tied to the political aims of the New Games movement and its Situationist older siblings, but is unabashedly about politics, and while it involves plenty of physical play with others, it's facilitated by technology (cell phones). One might call Re:Activism Dérive-meets-Pokémon Go, where 50 or so players in teams run around the city, discovering historic activist sites and play at protesting. Communications with teams are managed by "Re:Activism Central," where missions, team progress, and other game states are managed by facilitators via simple text messaging.

In the spirit of New Games, it's an extremely active game, often involving odd behaviors like lying on the busy sidewalks of Wall Street with one's eyes closed in a reenactment of a 1987 "die in" by Act Up, or chanting slogans from a 1915 suffragette march on Fifth Avenue. To play Re:Activism is to experience the vulnerability and power of collective bodies in action, as well as the puzzled gaze of pedestrians, unsure of whether this is a real protest or simply odd behavior. The players are following one set of rules, while passers-by are following another. When worlds and rules collide, funny things happen.

Sometimes, Re:Activism players encounter non-players actually protesting. At the Philadelphia edition of Re:Activism, players quit the game and joined an Occupy march underway. In New York, a team re-enacting the 1969 Stonewall Riots met some people who were actually present at that fateful summer night that sparked the LGBTQ rights movement, so they also quit the game, and retired to the historic bar to have beers and exchange stories. That team lost the game – but did they? One of the lessons from these two examples is that play and politics can easily morph. By playing at protest, players happened upon these moments – joining a protest, or enjoying stories of protest over some convivial beers. In other words, the players turned playing at protest into play as protest. Perhaps most importantly, they changed the game to suit their interests – coliberation! The key to coliberation, as DeKoven describes it, is the ability for players to change the rules of the game.[21]

Which brings us to protests of the present day – an activity on the rise in the US and around the world as political "strongmen" set rules that are decidedly not fun for everyone. In the US since the 2016 election, people who have never protested before have taken up placards and marched in the streets. But, as our playful guru DeKoven said recently, "don't worry about politics so hard that you forget how fun politics can be. Even, or maybe especially, public protest."[22]

Casual Games for Protestors is a collection of games one can play while actually protesting. Game designer Paolo Pedercini and artist Harry Giles—both also longtime activists—were worried about how long new activists could stay engaged before the inevitable protest fatigue wears in. This concern parallels Brand's observation a generation before that the activists he was working with "were starting to project a heaviness on a personal level that was just as bad as the heaviness we were projecting in Vietnam."[23] The antidote Pedercini/Giles and Brand came up with: games and play.

One of the *Casual Games for Protesters*, The Blame Game, puts protesters into the role of politicians, blaming the player to the left of some wrongdoing. This goes on "until everyone has been blamed for something at least three times, or until war breaks out." The game Medic models protest etiquette, providing a list of useful items to bring to a protest ("water, energy bars, painkillers, tampons, burner phones"), awarding points when an item is given away. And Microdisobedience turns any moment into a protest: "For the course of the day, disobey every rule you see written down or hear spoken, whether or not you disagree with it. Score a point for each rule you encounter and break. Which days and places have the most rules?"[24]

Microdisobedience is the penultimate game in this short history. It uncovers the rules underlying daily life, and encourages us to break them. Microdisobedience highlights the double-bind of all of the games explored so far: play in public is political when its rules enable the freedom to either break or change the rules of a public space – whether these rules are written or unwritten, explicit or implied, spatial or social. When we play, we create a temporary world within the real world, applying new rules and meaning to things – from streets to parachutes.

Play in public empowers us to change the rules of how we act in public, recreating, transforming, and breaking them. For a moment, we create a new, imaginary city atop the city. From games as protests (New Games, the Situationists) to games about protests (Re:Activism) and protests as games (*Casual Games for Protestors*), play morphs into political action and back again as it traverses public space. We become coliberated, if just for a moment, from everyday rules by playing in public. As DeKoven says: "Rules are made for the convenience of those who are playing. What is fair at one time or in one game may be inhibiting later on. It's not the game that's sacred, it's the people who are playing."[25] I recently asked DeKoven if this statement, from his book *The Well-Played Game*, had double-meaning. In other words, was he talking not just the rules of a game, but the rules we live by? And he simply said, "Bingo."[26]

Challenges:

ⓘ Interview - Ask a passerby why the Stonewall Tavern holds historical signifigance in the struggle for gay rights. *Document with video.*

ⓟ Protest - Get your team to sing the "The Stonewall Girls" song heard on the night of the riots. For added flair perform it cabaret style as it was at the riot, complete with high kicks! *Document with video and/or pictures*

"We are the Stonewall Girls, we wear our hair in curls,
We always dress with flair, we wear clean underwear,
We wear our dungarees, above our nellie knees,
We ain't no wannabees, we pay our Stonewall fees!"

ⓡ Reenactment - Stage an improvised reenactment of the riot scene from the beginning raid to the angry blockade. *Document with video.*

1 Indiecade, "A Conversation with Eric Zimmerman and Bernie DeKoven" (IndieCade 2012), https://youtu.be/Wr6b3_sFMCs (accessed January 20, 2018).

2 New Games Foundation & Andrew Fluegelman (ed.), *The New Games Book* (New York: Dolphin Books/Doubleday & Co., 1976).

3 Ibid., 10–11.

4 Ibid., 7–8.

5 Ibid., 8.

6 Ibid., 9.

7 Ibid., 9.

8 Bernard DeKoven, "The Politics of Public Playfulness," *TedX Asheville* (2015), https://www.youtube.com/watch?v=FnG3-k5phUM (accessed January 30, 2018).

9 Bernard De Koven, "Coliberation," *Deep Fun*, https://www.deepfun.com/coliberation/ (accessed January 30, 2018).

10 Fred Turner, "Why Study New Games," *Games & Culture* 1, no. 1 (2006): 1–4.

11 Guy Debord, "Theory of the Dérive," *Les Lèvres Nues 9* (1956), trans. Ken Knabb, http://www.cddc.vt.edu/sionline/si/theory.html (accessed March 5, 2018).

12 Ibid.

13 Constant Nieuwenhuys, *New Babylon – a Nomadic City* (The Hague: Haags Gemeetemuseum, 1974).

14 Described in detail Colleen Macklin & John Sharp, *Games, Design and Play: A Detailed Approach to Iterative Game Design* (New York: Addison-Wesley, 2016).

15 Katie Salen & Eric Zimmerman, *Rules of Play: Game Design Fundamentals*, (Cambridge: MIT Press, 2003), 168.

16 Ian Borden, *Skateboarding, Space and the City: Architecture and the Body* (Oxford, UK: Berg Publishers, 2001).

17 See the work of Raoul Bunschoten and his lab, CHORA.

18 National Park Service Department of the Interior, Golden Gate National Recreation Area, "2017 Superintendent's Compendium of Designations, Closures, Permit Requirements and Other Restrictions Imposed Under Discretionary Authority," https://www.nps.gov/goga/learn/management/upload/2017-Compendium.pdf (accessed January 30, 2018).

19 Johan Huizinga, *Homo Ludens: A Study of the Play-Element in Culture* (London: Routledge & Kegan Paul, 1949), 10.

20 For more information, see http://colleenmacklin.com/reactivism.

21 Bernard DeKoven, *The Well-Played Game: A Player's Philosophy* (Cambridge: MIT Press, 1978) 47.

22 Bernard DeKoven, "The Playful Practice: Maybe the Most Politically Relevant Thing You Can Do is to Keep On Playing" (March 16, 2017), https://www.deepfun.com/playful-practice-maybe-the-most-politically-relevant-thing-you-can-do-is-to-keep-on-playing/ (accessed January 30, 2018).

23 New Games Foundation & Fluegelman, *The New Games Book*, 8.

24 "Casual Games for Protesters," http://www.protestgames.org/ (accessed March 5, 2018).

25 DeKoven, *The Well-Played Game*, 44.

26 Phone interview with author (November 13, 2017).

IN CONVERSATION WITH
PAOLA ANTONELLI

Paola Antonelli is senior curator of architecture and design, and director of research and development, at the Museum of Modern Art (MoMA) in New York City. She is on a mission to introduce–and explain–design to the world. In 2015, she was recognized with an AIGA Medal for "expanding the influence of design in everyday life by sharing fresh and incisive observations and curating provocative exhibitions at MoMA." Antonelli has been rated one of the 100 most powerful people in the world of art by *Art Review* and *Surface Magazine*, and one of the 25 most incisive design visionaries by *Time Magazine*. **Daniel Pittman** interviewed Antonelli in New York on behalf of *LA+ Journal*.

"Victimless Leather" by Oron Catts and Ionat Zurr –
a miniature coat grown from mouse stem cells, from
Design and the Elastic Mind, MoMA (2008).

+ I am intrigued by your statement, "It is important to stay relevant and to look to museums as the R&D of society." What kind of R&D does MoMA do?

PA With R&D, one of the initiatives that was started right away were the salons. We've had 23 of them, and they have covered topics ranging from culture and metrics, to taboos, death, truth, and the changed role of the objects in the world today. These themes are at the same time philosophical and very real in the sense that they are central and important to every human being.

We are exploring the role of museums as engaged in helping society and citizens deal with important matters in their life, by offering art as a place for experimenting, thinking, and having discussions at a more active and inspiring level. That's the kind of research that MoMA does. It's research about the human dimension, the human condition. That's what artists really do, too. They explore and dig deep into our nature, warts and all, and help us understand it so that we can build a more human and humane future.

+ You have spoken of your curatorial stance having to evolve with technological change. What kinds of technological change are you currently interested in and why?

PA I've always been interested in technology; I got my degree in architecture from a polytechnic, so I was very close to people in the engineering department. I believe that technology is the foundation that gives the reality check, spice, and true sense of possibility to architecture and design. The difference between design and art is that design has to be reality based – even when it's speculative, it always emanates from reality.

I've always loved the grounding of technology, and I believe that design is the enzyme that makes innovation happen. Scientific revolutions, historical upheavals, and technological discoveries would not become part of our lives without designers. Designers are the ones that can take the internet when it's still lines of code and give it an interface that makes it usable by everyone. Designers are the ones that take innovations like AR [augmented reality], or even something like microwaves, and create objects that make the technology usable. Of course, they collaborate with engineers all the time, but the last step, the last connection is made by the designers; so, technology and design go hand in hand.

Augmented reality interests me – I like the fact that it doesn't detach you completely from reality. I'm also very much interested in 3-D printing, but not just as an artistic medium. Rather, I'm interested in the kind of 3-D printing that can also be achieved with biological materials. I'm interested in the wet revolution. I'm interested in how biology is front and center in the world of engineering and of design right now. I'm working on a new project that is called "Broken Nature" for the next Triennale di Milano. It's based on the idea of restorative design – design that tries to reconnect some of the severed threads that we have with nature at all scales. There's a lot of biodesign in it.

Above: Installation view from "Items: Is Fashion Modern?" MoMA (2017).

PA I work with a general theory of design that I apply to different fields. For example, I think of bio-bricks and code as the same kinds of tools as real bricks. Even though the theory and the approach might be the same, the outcome is different because the potential that these tools offer are completely different. Good design happens when you set goals and then use the means at your disposal in an economical, efficient, and elegant–even formally elegant–way. Though the realms are different, and the goals might be different, the way I evaluate design is always the same. How did you get to the goal that you set out for us, and does this goal add something to the world?

It might seem very theoretical, but if you go through some examples, you realize that it is a quite sensible set of criteria that can be used by every human being. I believe that my role as a curator is not to tell people what is good or bad, but rather to help them fine-tune their own critical tools.

+ Do you see a continuity or consistency in how you treat these different technologies or does each create their own opportunities?

PA I don't think there's anything reassuring, no. It is exciting, and it's also fearful. I had a very strange experience a few years ago when I realized that design is not all for good. It can be for evil too. When I heard about the 3-D printed gun, I experienced a flow of emotions that went from being stunned to being angry at myself for being stunned, because, of course, whenever you do something, it can be used one way or the other.

The same happens with biodesign. There's something amazing about biodesign when it comes to ethics. It posits very deep questions, and it puts you as a human being in a state of crisis. It can provoke questions as simple as asking vegetarians if they would eat meat grown in vitro, delicious, normal-tasting meat, but harvested without touching an animal. I had a similar experience in 2008 when I did an exhibition called "Design and the Elastic Mind" that was about design in science. One piece ["Victimless Leather"] I showed in MoMA was an object of biodesign. It was in an incubator that nourished mouse stem cells to grow over a scaffold of proteins in the shape of a miniature coat. The designers Oron Catts and Ionat Zurr came to New York from Perth, Australia, and together with colleagues from Columbia University, set everything up for the exhibition. After a few weeks though, the coat was growing in a strange way. A sleeve was too long. It was growing too big and clogging the incubator.

So, I contacted Oron and Ionat in Australia and explained what was happening. They said, "Well, you know what? It's not growing well. You have to stop the incubator." I told them, "One second. That would mean killing the coat." And they explained, "No, no, it was never alive." Even though I've always had firm beliefs about abortion rights, I really had a hard time killing–I thought at first it was killing–that coat. It compels you to think about it long and hard.

+ You mentioned the wet revolution and biodesign earlier; is designing life the next frontier? Should we be reassured, or should we be afraid?

This year is *Frankenstein*'s 200th anniversary, and it's a big deal. Not only in the world of movies and fantasy, but also in the world of biodesign. The ethical implications are truly deep, and that's what biodesign does – it allows us, when it's speculative, to really ask ourselves questions. Then of course, when it is directly applied and becomes reality, it's out of our control.

I'm sure that there are things happening in labs and universities all over the world that would scare the bejesus out of us, but at the same time, there's not much that we can do. I don't think that anyone could ever have a magic wand and make evil, or even just misguidedness, disappear from Earth. We should be afraid, but in the same way we should have been afraid five centuries ago.

+ Your contributions to MoMA's permanent collection are famous and varied–the @ sign, ancient algorithms–what would you add if you could?

PA One of my obsessions (that now is actually becoming impossible) is to acquire a Boeing 747, but without having the plane here at MoMA, instead letting it fly. The problem is that 747s are being grounded now, and it kills me because it's the dromedary of the skies. It's so beautiful. It really tears my heart. The idea was to keep it flying by making a deal with an airline – two or three aircraft that are used to fly through New York would be the MoMA ones. If you happened to take a MoMA flight, you would get a special boarding pass that would point you towards the amazing design details on the 747. You would also be able to take a 10-minute guided tour before the plane took off that points out all these different features. The plane would have the same configuration as other 747s, because that's a design choice, but maybe a different upholstery fabric and re-edited cutlery. Then maybe too the onboard store would sell MoMA design store items. It was this beautiful construct, but I know it's never going to happen. Just having these discussions is so fascinating to me because it makes you wonder what the job of a curator is.

I believe that the job of a curator is varied – there are different kinds of curators. In the case of art, it's important for museums to own the art, take responsibility and be accountable, because art often comes in a unique form. But, when it comes to design, we can also just produce lists. For instance, we did an exhibition in 2004 called *Humble Masterpieces*, and the whole premise was that we could have an exhibition with these objects, but in a way, you could have your own collection too. The show included things like Post-It notes, Chupa Chups, Jelly Beans, staplers, and the brown paper bag. These are masterpieces of design, but they're humble masterpieces that you also have at home.

Design is a wonderful part of a museum like MoMA because as the founding director, Alfred Barr, said many, many years ago, design was the opportunity that everyone had to have art in their lives. At that time, they equated art with design and design with art. To me, design is not art, but still, it's a beautiful field of human creativity. It's even more beautiful because it can be had by many.

+ Your exhibitions are often framed with explicit acknowledgement of complexity and context. Is this going to be increasingly the norm given the material that you are dealing with?

PA I think it has to become more of the norm. It's not yet. There are many museums and curators of design that still think of the object as disconnected from its context, but it's changing. It's changing in an irresistible way – in all kinds of philosophical or cultural studies, the idea of context has become fundamental. When you think of context in terms of design, the context is the whole system of production: the sourcing of materials, the design, manufacturing, and also the life cycle. It's what happens to design when it is no longer in use and is being recycled or biodegrading. It really is important to remain conscious of the fact that an object is not coming from outer space. It's something that has a past, a present, and a future.

PA It's interesting because the most advanced designers and architects are the ones that have understood that the world is not an object of design, but rather that the world is a designer. There are many architects and designers who are trying to learn from nature's processes, or even coopt nature to grow objects and buildings, as opposed to design them from the top down. The realization of how we have imposed our will on the planet has led some really interesting designers to look at things from the other viewpoint.

I don't think that any category of thinkers or doers can save the world. First of all, I'm not even sure that the world needs saving. Maybe the best way would be for us to become extinct, and then the world would go on by itself to a better future. I think that we can all work together though. Designers are very good at building interdisciplinary teams and at understanding issues and setting goals. I believe designers should be more central to policymaking, to governing, to projecting, and to thinking long term. They should definitely be used better, and they should position themselves better.

I don't know that it would save the world, but designers definitely could help our species design a better ending, so that the next dominant species will remember us with a little respect. I really believe that we should be better and that designers can help us be better because they have a certain clarity that is ethical, but also aesthetic. Aesthetics are a form of respect of human communication, so it's much deeper than one would think.

PA I would approach it by mixing digital and real. I think it would make it much more interesting. When I think of digital landscapes, I'm not just thinking of Second Life or video games. I'm also thinking of very simple WordPress sites, because I consider those environments and landscapes too. We need to recognize that we spend a lot of time in digital environments. Sometimes they are on the scale of interior designs, and other times they are as large as territories. We need to learn from the real world to also apply critical tools to the digital world.

Of course, there are great examples of landscape design all over the world, and they can be organized in an exhibition in a very thoughtful way, but I think that it would be most interesting to create bridges and connections and be intersectional. Maybe have trios of Western world, non-Western world, and digital, and give a taxonomy that always leads you through these three different dimensions.

+ So, if the planet is now an object of design, can design save the world?

+ Since MoMA's Rising Tides exhibition and the completion of major public works in New York, works of landscape architecture have been somewhat in the spotlight. If you were to put together an exhibition on the contemporary landscape, how would you approach it?

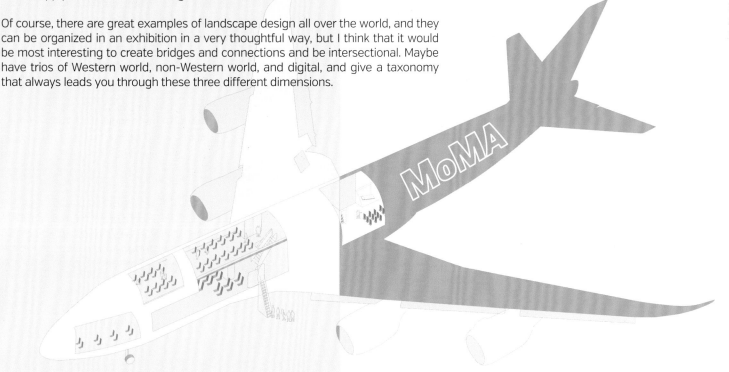

![Cover image for Warning Signals by David Salomon, a grainy black-and-white image resembling seismographic or sonar printout.](cover)

DAVID SALOMON
WARNING SIGNALS

David Salomon is the coordinator of the Architectural Studies program and an Assistant Professor of Art History at Ithaca College, New York. He has published and lectured widely on the relationship between architecture, landscape, and infrastructure. Salomon was co-curator and co-convener of the 2017 "Ambiguous Territory: Architecture, Landscape, and the Postnatural" exhibition and symposium held at the University of Michigan.

+ TECHNOLOGY, DESIGN

Red lights flash on a control room console. Horns blare across campuses and compounds. Shrill sounds followed by a mechanical voice are broadcast over the airwaves. A voice message, email, and text message are simultaneously sent out. These are the well-known and often perception-jarring techniques used to announce that an imminent environmental, technological, criminal, or geo-political risk is at hand. Such events include the failure of infrastructure grids, an impending storm, tsunami, flood, or tornado, a leak in a nuclear reactor, the presence of a criminal on a campus, an impending missile attack. These warnings are designed to effectively and immediately activate safety protocols–both personal and institutional–to keep populations protected, typically by prescribing where people can or cannot go and what they should and should not do. In other words, while their scope is territorial, their effects are architectural.

Early versions of such warning systems relied on room-sized computers and were monitored by men in clandestine control rooms, but we are now "observed" by billions of sensors that are instantaneously checked and controlled by impersonal algorithms.[2] Today's surveillance networks rely less and less on human or even mechanical modes of vision to do their jobs. The linked and automated systems of devices that are buried into or placed upon the Earth's surface respond to multiple forms of energy.[3] They communicate with each other at the speed of light and produce data that advise us about or warn us of the dangers and opportunities lurking in the coming seconds, minutes, hours, and days.

However, while military and weather-watching systems still monitor the heavens for atmospheric threats to our shared safety, today's monitoring devices are increasingly deployed for personal pleasure and profit. The initial goal of communal protection has been supplemented by the desire for individual economic and behavioral efficiency. What began as a method for monitoring rare "acts of God" or horrific acts of war has become the normative state of interacting with the marketplace. In other words, a technique for identifying risks has become one itself.

Surveillance systems have long been understood to come with their own set of unintended consequences. For centuries philosophers and artists have excitedly and earnestly pointed out the long-term social effects of surveillance technologies – from More's Utopia to Bentham's panopticon to Amazon's Alexa.[4] This reminds one that not all threats can be detected and resolved with more automation and speed. Some dangers move slower and require reflection and debate, as well as recursive data processing, to be resolved. Both the history and the future of geological [and geopolitical], climatic, social, and evolutionary changes operate at the scale of decades, centuries, and millennia and require solutions that recognize these different rates of change.

Today, as the physical environment increasingly comes under the influence of automated non-human agents, and, as the risks posed to the health of those environments are increasingly long-term ones, designers are faced with a dilemma: how to operate at the speed of micro-sensors and processors yet plan at the rate of evolutionary and geological time; how to effectively integrate a cascade of real-time information with eons of ecological insights? When contemporary architects, landscape architects, urban planners, and artists have engaged the temporal disjuncture between the speed of digital sensing and monitoring machines and the slow and long-term dangers posed by the Anthropocene in their design processes, they have taken one of three approaches: positivist, pragmatic, or projective.[5]

Opposite: Side-scan sonar anomaly, seafloor survey, NOAAS *Mt. Mitchell*, 1993.

Positivist Plans

The positivist position—taken up by organizations like the Breakthrough Institute and MIT's Senseable City Lab—holds that the best way to combat the ills created by industrial technology (e.g., pollution, resource depletion, social inequality) is by accelerating the role of information technologies into the design, construction, and inhabitation process. The implied positivist mantra being smarter is better.[6]

The threat it monitors and attempts to correct for is waste: of capital, of natural and human resources, and of data itself. This "eco-technical" or "eco-modernist" approach advocates for the increased use of digital monitoring devices to identify unwanted environmental effects and social behaviors, and to feed this data back into the system in order to remove said problems.[7] The advantages of this outlook are framed in terms of efficiency: economic, environmental, and social. This emphasis preserves the modernist/industrial methods of isolating and optimizing systems for specific outputs, and proposes to use advanced information gathering and processing technologies to maintain and expand current methods of wealth production without sacrificing environmental health.[8] This emphasis on maintaining the status quo is both indexed and symbolized by the fact that the devices and systems employed in such projects are almost always kept out of sight.

This position is embodied in new large-scale real estate developments such as Hudson Yards in New York, which will embed sensors to monitor the flow of water, trash, energy, information, and people. The data collected will be used in turn to reduce costs and energy use, but also to save time and energy for the residents living there by providing services from ultra-fast WiFi, to hyper efficient waste management, heating, and cooling systems. Everything, living or not, can be made more productive. And, every action by human and nonhuman agents is a source of information: information that is privately held and used and sold for profit.[9]

Within this ethos even sewage becomes an information-rich material. Building on studies in Europe that sought to identify locations of high recreational drug use by monitoring the drugs' chemical presence in city sewage systems,[10] MIT Senseable City Lab's "Underworlds" project uses a robot to identify the presence of certain bacteria in sewage systems.[11] This information would enable health officials to recognize and contain the outbreak of illnesses associated with the bacteria in real time. Of course, the same could be done for illegal drug usage. In both cases, the sensed data identifies and isolates bad actors (germs, drugs, people) from good ones by policing bodily waste.[12] Such a system echoes the goals, and the invisibility, of the original military surveillance systems, namely, that of keeping a certain set of bodies safe from others. As with many projects that heed a positivist approach to smart landscapes, for every benefit it seems to create it also brings one closer to the dystopian scenario of societal control via the ubiquitous and invisible monitoring of people and behaviors.[13]

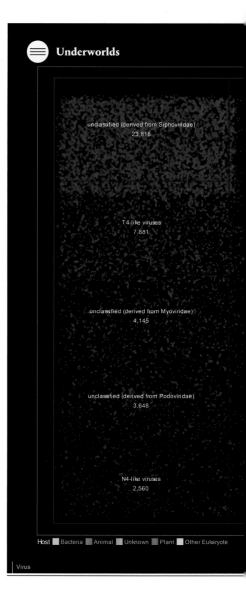

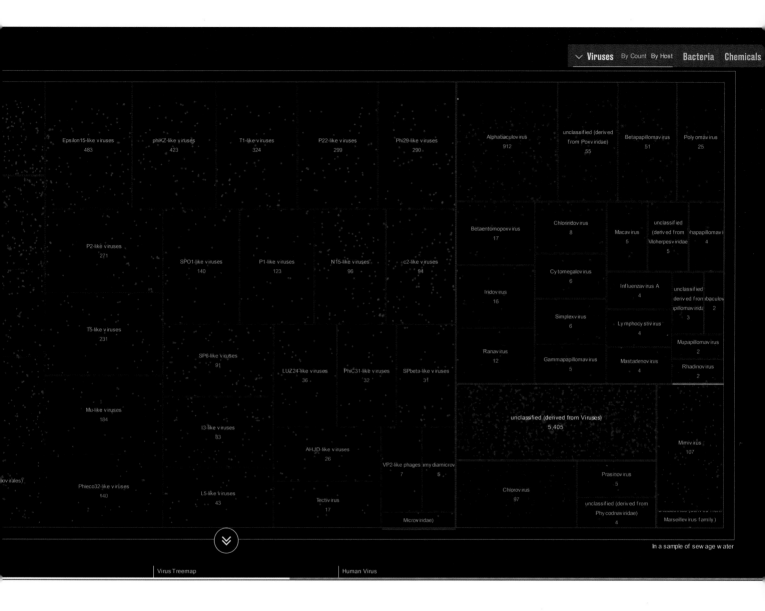

Epsilon15-like viruses
483

phiKZ-like viruses
423

T1-like viruses
324

P22-like viruses
299

Phi29-like viruses
290

Alphabaculovirus
912

unclassified (derived from Poxviridae)
55

Betapapillomavirus
51

Polyomavirus
25

P2-like viruses
271

SPO1-like viruses
140

P1-like viruses
123

N15-like viruses
96

c2-like viruses
94

Betaentomopoxvirus
17

Chloriridovirus
8

Macavirus
5

unclassified (derived from Alloherpesviridae)
5

Dhapapillomavir
4

Iridovirus
16

Cytomegalovirus
6

Influenzavirus A
4

unclassified derived from baculov
apillomavirida 2
3

T5-like viruses
231

Simplexvirus
6

Lymphocystivirus
4

Mupapillomavirus
2

SP6-like viruses
91

LUZ24-like viruses
36

PhiC31-like viruses
32

SPbeta-like viruses
31

Ranavirus
12

Gammapapillomavirus
5

Mastadenovirus
4

Rhadinovirus
2

Mu-like viruses
184

I3-like viruses
83

unclassified (derived from Viruses)
5,405

ov irales)

Phieco32-like viruses
140

L5-like Viruses
43

AHJD-like viruses
26

Tectivirus
17

VP2-like phages
7

rmy diamicrov
5

Mimivirus
107

Chlorovirus
97

Prasinovirus
5

unclassified (derived from Phycodnaviridae)
4

Marseillevirus family)

Microviridae)

Treemap of viruses in a sample of sewage water taken in Cambridge, MA. From "Underworlds," a project by the MIT Senseable City Lab and Alm Lab.

Pragmatic Positions

The pragmatic stance shares the positivist imperative to use accurate digital imaging and surveillance techniques to better document, understand, and intervene in existing urban and environmental conditions. However, rather than champion progress and profits, it recognizes the ability of these tools to reveal (and even produce) yet to be seen spatial narratives and behaviors. The environmental and social threats it exposes include the danger of acting in and on the world without understanding the underlying, interconnected but invisible facts (both physical and political) that guide it. It also serves to caution one against accepting existing conditions as inevitable or intractable. The future can be changed, it argues, but only if you accurately represent, understand, and communicate how the present works.

The pragmatic perspective operates on the spectrum of critical to productive. The critical approach challenges certain economic development practices by exposing the unexpected and unsettling environmental side effects of urbanization and resource extraction. The practitioners in the pragmatic group include photographer Edward Burtynsky and experimental filmmaker Liam Young. Their alluring but disturbing high-definition, large format, documentary images depict the "becoming ruin" of polluted landscapes and decaying urban sites.[14] These images are not optical photographs dependent on vision, instead they are images created by digital "multispectral scanning" machines that register environmental energy on an electrically charged surface and translate it into legible and easily manipulated representations.[15] These information-rich images function similarly to early environmental warning systems in that they do not prevent unwanted actions from taking place, rather, they warn us of invisible imminent dangers.

Practices that operate at the more instrumental end of the pragmatic spectrum look to directly intervene in the physical environment, but not before accurately documenting them first. Using a combination of electronically linked sensors that are located on the ground, underwater, in satellites, and mounted on drones, landscape architect Christophe Girot has pioneered the use of digital point clouds to generate accurate representations of existing environments.[16] These hyperreal, computationally dependent simulations allow designers to simultaneously predict the material behavior of the air, soil, and water on a site, and accurately model the perceptual effects these changes will produce. This opens up the design process to experimentation and recursion, as both physical limitations and sensorial effects can immediately be identified and either be abandoned or creatively overcome before construction begins.

"Datascape"–a project created by Yi Liu, Yitian Wang, and Matty A. Williams for the Synthetic Urban Ecologies studio run by Bradley Cantrell in 2013–proposes an alternative way of acting on social-spatial behavior.[17] At first glance it is a simple scheme for monitoring and representing atmospheric conditions in West

Oakland, California; however, its true agenda is to influence how, when, and where people use the city. It proposes to do so by harnessing information on the presence of particulate matter and its sources from existing public sensors and augmenting it with on-the-ground data uploaded by users. It would then communicate these atmospheric conditions back to the residents of Oakland via an augmented map interface. This real-time map would illustrate how one could occupy and circulate through the city using the "cleanest" routes. In other words, without adding any physical architectural or infrastructural elements, spatial behaviors could be changed. Like the other examples illustrating the pragmatic approach, "Datascape" captures environmental information to produce alternative realities rather than optimized ones.

Projective Play

The projective approach to incorporating information technologies into natural and physical environments is a less direct, less "useful," and more disruptive one. It deviates the most from the normative logics of efficiency and/or profit associated with contemporary surveillance systems. It does so by introducing inefficient playful and random delays and detours into these systems' otherwise instrumental logics to create positive, rather than negative, feedback loops. In short, it is closer to art than design.

The threat the projective position identifies is the danger of passively accepting invasive information monitoring and processing networks as obvious markers of progress. It does so not by didactically pointing out the pitfalls of the surveillance state, but by embedding conceptual and aesthetic blind spots within it. In doing so it advances the skepticism about surveillance long held by many authors, artists, designers, and philosophers. This group, perhaps because of their recognition of the dependence of messages on the media used to send them, has been quick to recognize the specter of censorship–both verbal and spatial–underlying the intensive monitoring and aggregation of information.[18]

Despite its skeptical stance, this is not a reactionary position. Projects that exhibit this point of view actively make use of the same advanced digital scanning, sensing, processing and modeling tools. However, they use them to create playful but no less serious spatial interventions. Diller Scofidio's Blur Building from 2002 is canonical in this regard. The ostensible goal of the project was to create a permanent cloud (created by a system of high-pressure pumps and nozzles) around an ovoid-shaped structure set in Lake Neuchâtel, Switzerland. Sensors constantly monitored the wind, humidity, and temperature and fed that information back to the misting machine. However, the system would only adjust itself every eight minutes, thus producing a lag between the creation of the fog and the environmental conditions it met. Instead of creating a negative feedback loop that would keep the shape of the cloud as consistent as possible, a positive feedback loop was established that was at once responsive to the context but also out of sync with it. While the onboard sensors, processors, and pumps could easily have kept up with the ever-changing microclimate around the Blur Building, the simple act of slowing down the feedback loop between environment and object highlights how limiting the logic of optimization is, how easy it is to disrupt it, and how unexpected the results can be when one does.[19]

A more conventionally functional but still playful example of using sensors, machines, air, and water to create unexpected spatial experiences is found in Philippe Rahm and Catherine Mosbach's design for Jade Eco Park in Taichung, Taiwan. The park was imagined as an environmental oasis for that hot and humid city. The distribution of pavilions and paths was governed by the specific climatic conditions already present on the former airport site, with each pavilion being programmed to sense the presence of a specific ambient condition (sunlight, heat, humidity, pollution, pests) and mediate its negative effects by introducing mechanically supplied water, air, or sound. Spaces are made more inviting by changing the environmental qualities rather than changing the architecture. As with the Blur Building, the goal was not to provide a homogeneous atmospheric effect or

1 Marshall McLuhan, "The Media is the Message" in *Understanding Media: The Extensions of Man* (New York: McGraw Hill, 1964) 9.

2 For a description of one of the earliest monitoring sites, NORAD's SAGE computer system, see John Harwood, "The White Room: Eliot Noyes and the Logic of the Information Age Interior," *Grey Room* 12 (2003): 7–31. For the history of infrastructure control rooms, see Shannon Mattern, "Mission Control: A History of the Urban Dashboard," *Places Journal* (March 2015). For a recent take on the coming age of algorithms, see Yuval Noah Harari, *Homo Deus: A Brief History of Tomorrow* (New York: Harper, 2017), 356–402. For the implications of artificial intelligence for architecture and landscape, see generally "Posthuman," *New Geographies* 9 (2017).

3 On the history of digital imaging and scanning techniques, see John May, "Everything is Already an Image," *Log*, no. 40 (2017): 9–26.

4 For an overview of surveillance, see Peter Marks, *Imagining Surveillance: Eutopian and Dystopian Literature and Film* (Edinburgh: Edinburgh University Press, 2015).

5 Etienne Turpin, ed., *Architecture in the Anthropocene: Encounters Among Design, Deep Time, Science and Philosophy* (Ann Arbor: Open Humanities Press, 2013).

6 Neil Brenner & Christian Schmid, "Towards a New Epistemology of the Urban?" *City* 19 (2015): 151–82.

7 Simon Guy & Graham Farmer, "Reinterpreting Sustainable Architecture: The Place of Technology, *Journal of Architectural Education* 54, no. 3 (2001): 140–48; Breakthrough Institute, *An Ecomodernist Manifesto*, http://www.ecomodernism.org/manifesto-english/.

8 As the Breakthrough Institute puts it: "We believe that human prosperity and an ecologically vibrant planet are possible at the same time." Breakthrough Institute, "Mission," https://thebreakthrough.org/about/mission/.

9 Shannon Mattern, "Instrumental City: The View from Hudson Yards, Circa 2019," *Places Journal* (April 22, 2016).

Opposite: Still from *Where the City Can't See* (2016), a video by Liam Young made using laser scanning technology.

idealized image; rather, the objective was to create distinct and ever-changing ambient zones around the pavilion that one would experience in a more tactile than visual way. While the structures themselves remain stable, the space defined by them, and the effects produced by them are in constant, and constantly surprising, flux.[20]

If the Blur Building and Jade Eco Park respond at the pace of microprocessors, Smout Allen and Geoff Manaugh's "L.A. Recalculated" moves at the speed of sludge. As represented in their "distributed cartographic drawing – part map, part plan, part deep section," their scheme distributes a set of awkward and out-of-scale "instruments" around Los Angeles. The deliberate movement of their exposed, infrastructure-sized gears and pulleys echo the lethargic pace of the tectonic, astrological, and hydrocarbon activity they sense and register. Some of the devices depicted might be for passive energy production and others could capture fossil fuels, but these are not their main functions. Rather, these joyful yet imposing giants monitor and monumentalize the dramatic difference between the unhurried physical processes that take place above and below the city's surfaces, and the chaotic human activity that takes place upon it, activities which are increasingly subjected to positivist modes of surveillance. Far from efficient, the toy-like forms and colors of these functional follies reveal both the innocence and the interest we have regarding the unseen, unrelenting, and operative processes and products that threaten and enable (e.g., earthquakes and crude oil respectively) our contemporary culture. The sense of awe and wonder these spectacular yet monstrous contraptions create doesn't veil this reality, rather, it exposes the simultaneous presence of dread and optimism that we hold about the present and future but very rarely express.[21]

Conclusion

The devices depicted in "L.A. Recalculated," as well as the Blur Building and Jade Eco Park, may be able to quantify and measure things and events, but these projective projects don't optimize any function or maximize profits. They do, however, do something: they serve as previews of an alluring yet unnerving future.

One might say the same about the positivist and pragmatic positions. However, they are attractive and unsettling for different reasons and ultimately have different goals. All three approaches presented are adept at identifying social and/or environmental threats and each suggests spatial strategies for guarding against them. Still, the positive and pragmatic strategies also embody the now normative belief that the increase in knowledge and productivity made possible by digital machines and methods can help us mitigate (but not remove) the unwanted side effects of informational and industrial technologies. Like the first generation of early warning systems they recognize when danger is present but they cannot prevent it from happening in the first place. They don't challenge the underlying causes of risk, they only address their symptoms.

In contrast, the projective stance seeks to augment current conditions with alternative situations, ones that don't directly solve problems as much as posit new questions, questions such as: Should information driven technologies always be efficient and productive? Should infrastructure be beautiful? This approach often produces artifacts and scenarios that may seem more like art and less like design. This doesn't make them any less useful. As Marshall McLuhan argued, the imagined worlds artists create today are the literal worlds the rest of us will be living in tomorrow.[22] In other words, artists function as different kinds of detection devices, ones that are able to both accurately assess the present in order to create new ways of acting in and on the future. If that is the case, then you can consider yourself warned.

10 Christoph Ort, et al., "Spatial Differences and Temporal Changes in Illicit Drug Use in Europe Quantified by Wastewater Analysis," *Addiction* 109 (2014): 1338–52, cited in Nicola Davis, "The MIT Lab Flushing Out a City's Secrets," *The Guardian* (March 27, 2016).

11 MIT Senseable City Lab, "Underworlds," http://underworlds.mit.edu (accessed May 13, 2018).

12 Davis, "The MIT Lab Flushing Out a City's Secrets."

13 Cynthia Graber, "Why an MIT Robot is Collecting Poop from Our Sewers," *Boston Globe Magazine* (January 19, 2017).

14 Jennifer Peeples, "Toxic Sublime: Imaging Contaminated Landscapes," *Environmental Communication: A Journal of Nature and Culture* 5, no. 4 (2011): 373–92.

15 John May, "Preliminary Notes on the Emergence of Statistical-Mechanical Geographic Vision," *Perspecta* 40 (2008): 42–53.

16 Christophe Girot & Philipp R.W. Urech, "Simulations as Model," *LA+ Interdisciplinary Journal of Landscape Architecture*, no. 4 (2016): 50–57.

17 "Datascape," in Bradley Cantrell & Justine Holtzman (eds) *Responsive Landscapes* (New York: Routledge, 2016), 112–17.

18 Among the more prescient philosophical discussions of digital modes of surveillance, see Paul Virilio, *Lost Dimension*, trans. Daniel Moshenberg (Semiotext(e), 1991), 9–27; and Gilles Deleuze, "Postscript on the Societies of Control," *October* 59 (1992): 3–7.

19 Ashley Schafer, "Designing Inefficiencies," in Aaron Betsky (ed.), *Scanning: The Aberrant Architectures of Diller + Scofidio* (New York: Whitney Museum of American Art, 2003), 92–102.

20 "The Performative Park," in Jillian Walliss & Heike Rahmann (eds), *Landscape Architecture and Digital Technologies: Re-conceptualizing Design and Making* (New York: Routledge, 2016).

21 Smout Allen & Geoff Manaugh, "L.A. Recalculated," *MAS Context*, no. 28 (2015).

22 McLuhan, "The Media is the Message," ibid.

Opposite: Massive subterranean pendulums that would act as earthquake counterbalances, from the "distributed cartographic drawing" by Smout Allen and Geoff Manaugh for their "L.A. Recalculated" project (2015).

CLAUDIA BODE + LIZZIE YARINA
DESIGN AS (RE-)ASSEMBLAGE

Claudia Bode is a Berlin-based architect and a research affiliate at the MIT Urban Risk Lab. She co-founded and directs the Kujenga Collaborative, an international group of designers, engineers, and makers invested in exploring the relationships between design and development in rural Tanzania. She holds a Master of Architecture from MIT and her writings on rurality, representation, and alternative urbanisms have been featured in a number of design journals and the book *Infrastructure Space* (2017).

Elizabeth (Lizzie) Yarina is a research associate with the MIT Urban Risk Lab. In 2017, she was a visiting Fulbright researcher at the Victoria University of Wellington, New Zealand, where she studied the spatial implications of climate change induced displacement. She holds a joint Master of Architecture and Master of City Planning from MIT and has published widely on the role of design thinking in territorial politics and climate risk.

+ PHILOSOPHY, DESIGN

Architecture is a complex and political act, embedded with historic bias and contemporary hegemony; the creation of spaces implicates hidden power structures and (im)material flows.[1] If "entire systems...the planet, and even the space beyond"[2] are now design problems, then grappling with them requires not only a reconception of design methods, but a new way of knowing the world: a design philosophy. Spatial designers need tools to understand how our interventions are connected to a complex, broad reality that doesn't end with disciplinary boundaries. As we are asked—or ask ourselves—to engage with the "super-wicked problems"[3] of the contemporary era (climate change, structural inequality, rapid urbanization) we also need an intellectual framework that allows us to engage with "things" that exceed our traditional ways of comprehending the world. Through an exploration of contemporary metaphysics examined in two contrasting design cases, we can start to uncover new tools for designers who are trying to navigate an increasingly interconnected, unknowable world.

Simplicity

While people have been designing objects, spaces, and landscapes for millennia, the codification of these activities into coherent disciplines is a more recent phenomenon related in part to the politics of nation-states. Design played a central role in the 19th and 20th centuries as the testing ground for ideologies of scientific progress; it was used as a tool in wide-ranging attempts to organize, simplify, and codify the world (through taxonomies, organization procedures, management systems) such that it could be comprehended and therefore controlled by European (colonial) states. The tendency towards simplicity or "legibility" as a hallmark of 20th-century thought is illustrated by political scientist and anthropologist James C. Scott.[4] According to Scott, the demands of modern statehood required the development of a new kind of biopolitics: new strategies to inventory goods, people, and resources were necessary in order to take on (and levy taxes to fund) ever more ambitious projects. An early example was the advent of scientific forestry in 18th-century Germany,[5] in which the nascent state created vast managed forests to extract a specific good (lumber). In the 20th century, exponentially more powerful colonial states deployed armies of bureaucrats, architects, planners, and builders to create brand new cities out of thin air; the prototypical example is Brasilia, conceived by Lucio Costa in 1957 as an homage to High Modernist architecture. Architectural quality notwithstanding, the process of creating Brasilia is a case study for the kind of top-heavy, *tabula rasa* urban planning later denounced by urbanist Jane Jacobs.[6]

High Modernist city making and German scientific forestry both represent attempts to simplify complex realities into something clear enough to be comprehended by a bureaucrat. An old-growth forest, with its myriad micro-habitats, ecological networks, and livelihood functions is not truly simple or legible, just as an urban system is an infinitely complex assemblage of culture, politics, ecologies, desires, and infrastructures that defies easy categorization. As Borges reminds us, we cannot create a 1:1 model of either environment.[7] Bracketing out the complexity of these systems is almost always a failure, whether as a result of the collapse of managed forests (due to lack of nutrient input from decomposing materials), or lack of spatial provisions for informal gathering and laborers in planned cities. Just as responsible forest management now ensures the existence of a diversity of species and habitats to prevent catastrophic ecological collapse, city planners have increasingly embraced the lessons of Jane Jacobs and others who saw the value of complexity over formal clarity: Jacobs's theory of "organized complexity" explains cities as "organisms that are replete with unexamined but obviously intricately interconnected, and surely understandable, relationships."[8]

The emphasis on simplicity or legibility in the modern episteme also affects the way we understand our own disciplines. Legibility came at the expense of *metis*, or practical, learned knowledge: this is what Marx referred to as the "de-skilling" of the proletariat.[9] In agricultural reform projects, for instance, the newly professionalized discipline of scientific agriculture superseded old, yet highly effective, traditional methods, such as permaculture or shifting cultivation, often at great cost.[10] Similarly, the architect who drew the initial sketches for the plan of Brasilia's "monumental axis" understood it as an abstract formal exercise, unconcerned with local ecologies, cultures, or climates.[11] As Jacobs contends: "The theorists of conventional modern city planning have consistently mistaken cities as problems of simplicity and of disorganized complexity, and have tried to analyze and treat them thus."[12] These projects actively resisted the introduction of alternative epistemologies and narratives; all the components of a project needed to fit neatly together in the service of an easy-to-manage and easy-to-visualize larger goal. Complex systems embedded in these spaces were bracketed out. By prioritizing legibility, the creators of these projects rejected disciplinary and epistemological mixing, handicapping themselves by excluding forms of knowledge that fell outside of narrowly defined worldviews.

Complexity

If the 20th century was marked in large part by this desire for comprehension and control, it is now undeniable that the world we have constructed is overwhelmingly complex. Globalization, the digital revolution, climate change, demographic pressures – these trends make change a constant aspect of our lives. If we look at catalysts–from the failure of Pruitt-Igoe, to the collapse of the Soviet Union, to the menacing specter of global terrorism and the changing face of war–it seems increasingly simplistic to assume that we ever really understood the whole picture. Maybe we've finally seen that a forest is not just a group of identical trees but some*thing* embedded with myriad intertwining histories, narratives, subjectivities.[13]

Philosopher Bruno Latour suggests that, in recognition of this reality, we should describe the objects around us as *things*. As Latour explains, the word "thing" has parallels in the Icelandic *Althing* (Parliament) and the Scandinavian *ding* (gathering).[14] Etymologically the term suggests that we consider objects (a building, a forest) not as singular objects but as assemblages: collections of ideas, materials, actions, and histories. Latour refers to the very complexity that is erased in the pursuit of legibility, and celebrates it: our entire existence is interwoven with such subjectivities, encompassing not only human thoughts, actions, beliefs, constructions, organizations, and cultures but also non-humans – animals, plants, what we often refer to as "Nature." When Latour famously claims that the split between culture and nature does not exist, he is questioning the isolation of objects: how could we neatly separate ourselves from our environment when we have in fact co-created it?[15] Titling our contemporary era as the "Anthropocene," even earth scientists are beginning to acknowledge that we are in an age where humans, through our production and extraction, have become a geologic force.

The ideas and methodologies of actor-network theory (ANT), expounded by Latour and other scholars of Science and Technology Studies, provide a framework for considering the myriad links between humans and nonhumans. They help illustrate the ways in which the objects in our world–in particular techno-scientific structures taken as essential or predetermined–are in fact both natural and social (semiotic) constructions. Importantly, in this framework, nonhumans (road signs, sandwiches, the Pythagorean theorem, walls, buildings, cities) also become actors.[16] Applying this theory to buildings, Latour and architectural anthropologist Albena Yaneva write, "Only by generating earthly accounts of buildings and design processes, tracing pluralities of concrete entities in the specific spaces and times of their co-existence, instead of referring to abstract theoretical frameworks outside architecture, will architectural theory become a relevant field for architects, for end users, for promoters, and for builders."[17]

While Bruno Latour's concept of the *thing* gives us a word for the infinitely complex and non-legible network that surrounds an object/concept (a *matter of concern* rather than a *matter of fact*),[18] fellow philosopher Timothy Morton shows how highly expansive, unknowable things are playing an increasingly important role in our universe. The world, and our conceptions of it, are dominated by these *hyperobjects*–such as climate change, the Internet, or the English language–which necessitate new forms of thought and action. Morton's view is that the world is fundamentally both illegible and highly interconnected. He describes climate change, for example, as a hyperobject that exists in a higher dimension we cannot access. We are only able to experience the bad photocopy: we feel rain on our heads, we notice the corals bleaching, we see the ice caps melting, but none of those things are, individually, climate change. We can never see it because "we can only see pieces of hyperobjects at a time,"[19] and while we might touch, relate to, or transform, or even be part of it, we remain distinct from it.

> Hyperobjects are thus like our experience of a pool while swimming. Everywhere we are submersed within the pool, everywhere the cool water caresses our body as we move through it, yet we are nonetheless independent of the water. We produce effects in the water like diffraction patterns, causing it to ripple in particular ways, and it produces effects in us, causing our skin to get goosebumps.[20]

In other words, hyperobjects are everywhere, around us and inside of us, never fully graspable. The things inside them form what Morton calls an *interobjective system* (a nonhuman form of intersubjectivity), a parallel concept to the actor-network. They are objects in relationship to one another, forming a *mesh*, as with the electrical wiring in a house.[21] The domains of spatial designers might too be seen as hyperobjects, particularly larger systems such as cities or landscapes. According to Morton, we can never "see" London, although we can catch a glimpse of particular streets, Trafalgar Square, specific people or events, or even an aerial perspective by satellite or helicopter: "London is not a whole that is greater than the sum of its parts. Nor is London reducible to those parts."[22]

Morton embraces complexity and illegibility: he would find it ludicrous to attempt to reduce a complex interobjective system

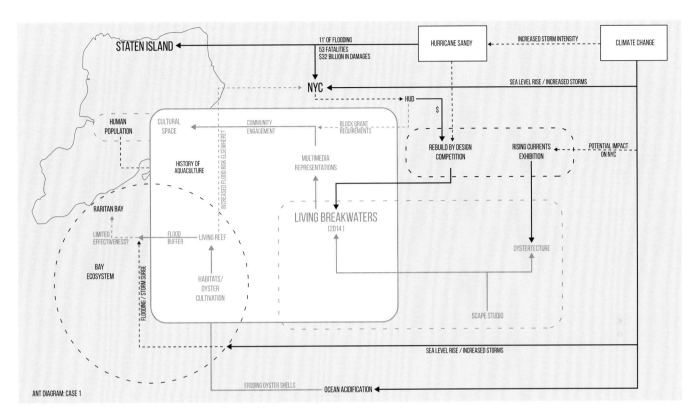

ANT DIAGRAM: CASE 1

like a forest to a neat summary. If we accept our design-space as irreducible, *things* and *hyperobjects* allow us to make decisions based on this infinite interconnectedness.

Design

Both Latour's and Morton's philosophical frameworks reflect the hyper-complex, hyper-networked reality that is referred to in the prompt for this issue. They provide a set of tools to comprehend the world we now live in: the Anthropocene, marked by severe ecological crisis and entirely new forms of global connectivity. By embracing multilayered complexity, they give designers an opportunity to move away from the long-standing limitations of legibility.

This is an opportunity, not a burden. Designers have agency that exists, in part, because we are generalists. We understand the big picture because we coordinate multiple specialists, desires, scales, and epistemologies in the service of a larger vision. Accepting complexity allows a project to include more of the elements of the system in which it operates; the project as thing or hyperobject emerges to engage multiple narratives and forms of agency. The definition of Brasilia, in this view, would include its sprawling squatter camps; the definition of the managed forest would include the many species of plants, animals, bacteria, and fungi that comprise a healthy ecosystem along with the human actors that rely upon forest products. Landscape architecture, always forced to contend with the inherent messiness that comes with designing within ecologies, would gain a vocabulary that allows it to describe more fully its embrace of complexity.

Designers, accustomed to the *metis*[23] of gathering and assembling, are better suited to this nonlinear methodology than more techno-scientific disciplines. But how does this work and what does this look like? What are the interobjective networks around a building, and a landscape, or other design propositions? Working backwards from a philosophical exploration of the world, *a la* Latour or Morton, how does design begin from and operate within a state of networked complexity?

The following two cases begin to dissolve the hard edges around disciplinary scope, beginning to approach the design project as a *thing* rather than an *object*. They are put in dialogue with each other because they are in many ways located on two ends of a spectrum: one, a well-known landscape architecture project situated firmly within the realm of design, the other a collection of individual designs, networks, and collaborations that arose in response to a single catalytic event. One is clearly authored, the other has many overlapping and even conflicting authors. Both are catalyzed by hurricane events and climate change's role in natural disaster, and make visible the potentials and pitfalls of attempting to work in and grasp these complex and unclear contexts.

Case 1: Building with Nature

Resilience projects that "build with nature" represent a trend toward understanding ecological systems as components of designed infrastructure. A well-known example is SCAPE Studio's "Oyster-tecture," a 2009 proposal for MoMA's *Rising Currents* exhibition, which evolved into their 2014 (and ongoing) "Living Breakwaters" design for the Rebuild By Design

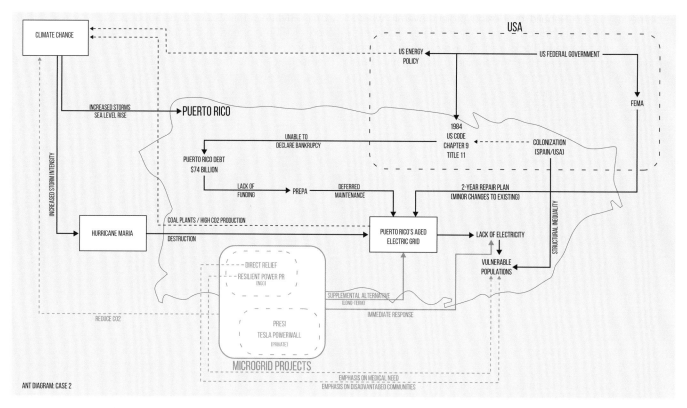

competition. Living Breakwaters centers around the use of oyster reefs as soft coastal buffers in Staten Island. The *parti* diagram for the project illustrates "risk reduction" in a reciprocal relationship with "ecology" and "culture"; urban environmental risk is expanded from a mere technical water issue to accommodate additional concerns. The breakwaters are part of a "thick section" including dunes and marshes which operate as buffers to coastal inundation, while also serving as a habitat for oysters, fish, clams, and other coastal biota. As shellfish encrust the below-sea breakwaters, they can grow upwards, adapting to increasing sea levels over time. This new "living infrastructure" draws on the area's long history of beach- and aqua-culture, while also creating new spaces for "shore-based communities."

SCAPE's project recognizes that, in preparing for the hyperobject of climate change, interventions *must* engage with these multiple spheres. The project operates as a counterpoint to singularly engineered solutions such as dikes and levees which treat rising seas as simply a technical problem of water management – water is a cultural and ecological object, and the project not only recognizes but directly engages with human and nonhuman actants. However, some critiques of the project suggest that even in this case, SCAPE may have not drawn the boundary widely enough. For oceans, one byproduct of anthropogenic changes to our atmosphere is increased ocean acidity, caused by CO_2 dissolved into sea waters. Increased acidity can dissolve the shells of mollusks, eroding the "living" component of the living breakwaters.[24] As a near-shore reef, the breakwaters' capacity to buffer against storm surge, one

of the most damaging impacts of Sandy, may also be limited.[25] The spatial extents of the project create a ripple of impacts as well. Any coastal infrastructure impacts the hydrodynamics of water systems around it: dikes, groynes, and breakwaters tend to speed up water flows and increase down-current erosion. Though the Living Breakwaters are "softer" than traditional concrete breakwaters, Ashley Dawson notes in Extreme Cities that the project still risks amplifying erosion across the bay in New Jersey.[26] Resilience projects, especially those that attempt to attenuate complex systems like ocean waves and currents, will always beg this question of how to draw the boundary around what is being protected by a project.

The potential of SCAPE's project lies in its embrace of a larger, messier *matter of concern* than what is usually seen in such projects – one which includes, in this case, animals performing the work of infrastructure. But while landscape architects (and, more recently, landscape urbanists) have long followed a McHargian line of thought that privileges the networked and the ecological, others would critique even this ecological expansion as insufficiently political, even post-political. "In the complex, sophisticated self-organizing, and evolutionary topographies drawn out by contemporary designers, political forces at work are obscured and structural ideas about social innovation are literally and figuratively displaced."[27] Here, on a (potentially) political level, the project *itself*–with its extensive publicity, emphasis on beautiful drawings, and accessibility to the public– forms a kind of social infrastructure that operates in parallel to what is actually constructed. This external engagement was fundamental to the Rebuild by Design project overall, where winning designers needed community buy-in in order to access Community Development Block Grant Disaster Recovery funds to realize their proposals. By transforming a dry, technocratic subject into something that engages and informs the public, the Living Breakwaters engages the cultural to help change national conversations about the necessity for flood defense as well as the perception of infrastructure itself: not a technocratic inevitability, but an opportunity for re-politicized discussion and design.

Case 2: Puerto Rican Microgrids

Hurricane Maria downed 80% of Puerto Rico's transmission and distribution lines, and the ensuing blackout has been the longest in American history. Many parts of the island are still without power, months later, and some households will remain in the dark for years. Even prior to the catastrophe of Maria, Puerto Rico's electricity system was struggling; $74 billion in debt ($9 billion by the power utility alone),[28] the territory could not afford to maintain the power grid. This debt must be understood in a post-colonial context: unlike mainland US states and cities that can declare bankruptcy when they've incurred unmanageable debt, as a non-state territory this option is unavailable.[29]

In response to the void created by the destruction of Puerto Rico's energy system, new, decentralized models are being proposed. Microgrids—autonomously functioning local energy systems with distributed power production—do not require the large-scale transmission infrastructure associated with traditional systems. The Puerto Rico Energy Security Initiative, for instance, is initially focusing on installing solar microgrids in places like hospitals and shelters where power is critical.[30] These renewable microgrid projects/proposals represent a "thinging" of electricity in Puerto Rico. Rather than seeing disaster response, infrastructure restoration, and infrastructure redesign as separate projects (where typically expensive and fuel-hungry emergency generators would stand in until the existing, already problematic energy system is repaired), with rapidly deployable microgrids both are resolved. Localized solar microgrids, if deployed correctly, would also be more resilient to future storms, as they don't rely on island-wide distribution networks.

In modern contemporary society, we often experience *adiaphorization*[31] with resources such as energy, meaning when we flip on a light switch, we rarely consider the systems that make electricity possible or where our power comes from; both the hurricane and these solar projects redefine relationships between people and infrastructure. Placing energy into local hands, these projects can also combat the degradation of public services due to austerity measures imposed as a result of Puerto Rico's debt. However, not all microgrid designs are created equally: relying on private companies such as Tesla to power up Puerto Rico may result in a prioritization of either those who can afford products like their $6,200 Powerwall (in a territory with an average household income under $20,000),[32] or who have needs which can easily attract donations (like the Hospital del Niño, where Tesla installed a solar array in October

2017). Private, rather than state support, lacks assurance of even distribution, and in a neoliberal model of infrastructure provision everyday Puerto Ricans may be expected to "pull themselves up by their bootstraps" and sort out their own energy supply concerns.

Projects like Resilient Power Puerto Rico (RPPR)[33] make the additional connections between energy provision and the complexity of postcoloniality and structural inequality, as ongoing power outages can put already disadvantaged communities even further behind. RPPR's phased proposal to install neighborhood relief hubs, municipal solar arrays, and household level solar panels recognizes the needs of multiple groups at varying scales. The localization of power also pushes back against the lack of control Puerto Ricans face as citizens of an American territory that cannot vote for the US president or congress. Similarly, rather than starting with the object (electricity), agencies like Direct Relief begin with complex hyperobjects like post-disaster health equity and work backwards to the role that sustainable solar electricity might play in keeping medicines refrigerated and dialysis machines running. Rather than allowing these to remain as traditionally discrete disciplines, thinking about healthcare and energy infrastructure in an integrated way creates opportunities to resolve both issues more equitably.

Unlike SCAPE's Living Breakwaters project, in Puerto Rico there is no clear *parti*. Here, the multiplicity of approaches that have sprung out of necessity during the emergency open doors that were long closed due to technological lock-in, political apathy, or lack of money. Potential energy providers are now being forced to consider factors—such as needs in the healthcare industry—they may have previously ignored, leading to new collaborations and broader thinking about the potential of an energy system to shape other aspects of society. Now, as Puerto Rico stares down the governor's attempts to privatize the electricity authority, understanding the interobjective ripples of a privately operated energy system is more important than ever.

Blur

The critiques embedded in the previous cases should indicate that their very interobjectivity makes them permanently imperfect: there is no "solution" to the hyperobject of climate change or hurricane risk and recovery. When success is not strictly bound by rigid disciplinary parameters there is always an opposing viewpoint. Their inclusion here, however, illustrates certain ways that the perimeters of the project could expand to absorb (and mediate) more of the messy realities of the world. As socio-political, environmental, and economic critiques of architecture and design suggest, bracketing out these other components of our reality risks a domino effect in these realms (i.e., the protestations over the AIA's public support of Trump's infrastructure plan, critiques of "starchitecture" as a tool for gentrification or neoliberal speculation,[34] or the massive steel consumption of Herzog and de Meuron's Bird's Nest Stadium). Design for the built environment can no more be depoliticized

1 Bruno Latour & Albena Yaneva, in Reto Geiser (ed.), "Give Me a Gun and I Will Make All Buildings Move: An ANT's View of Architecture," *Explorations in Architecture: Teaching, Design, Research* (Berne: Birkhauser, 2008): 80–89.

2 From the prompt for this issue.

3 Kelly Levin, et al., "Playing it Forward: Path Dependency, Progressive Incrementalism, and the 'Super Wicked' Problem of Global Climate Change," *International Studies Association 48th Annual Convention* (Chicago, 2007).

4 James C. Scott, *Seeing Like a State: How Certain Schemes to Improve the Human Condition Have Failed* (New Haven: Yale University Press, 1998).

5 Ibid.

6 Jane Jacobs, *The Death and Life of Great American Cities* (New York: Vintage, 2016).

7 J.L. Borges, "Of Exactitude in Science" (1946).

8 Jacobs, *The Death and Life of Great American Cities.*

9 Robert Stuart, *Marxism at Work: Ideology, Class and French Socialism During the Third Republic* (London: Cambridge University Press, 2002).

10 Scott, *Seeing Like a State.*

11 Ibid., 118.

12 Jacobs, *The Death and Life of Great American Cities*, 435.

13 In fact we now know that forests are networked super-organisms, communicating through their root structures through a fungal network in the forest floor. See, Monika A. Gorzelak, et al., "Inter-plant Communication through Mycorrhizal Networks Mediates Complex Adaptive Behaviour in Plant Communities," *AoB Plants* 7 (2015).

14 Bruno Latour, "Why Has Critique Run Out of Steam? From Matters of Fact to Matters of Concern," *Critical Inquiry* 30, no. 2 (2004): 225–48.

15 "It is now necessary to manage a single system of nature and of society": Bruno Latour, "To Modernize Or to Ecologize? That is the Question," in Kristin Asdal, Brita Brenna, and Ingunn Moser (eds.), *Technoscience: The Politics of Interventions* (Oslo: Unipub, 2007), 249–72.

16 Bruno Latour, *Reassembling the Social: An Introduction to Actor-Network-Theory* (Oxford: Oxford University Press, 2005), 10.

17 Latour & Yaneva, "Give Me a Gun and I Will Make All Buildings Move."

18 Latour, "Why Has Critique Run Out of Steam?"

19 Timothy Morton, *Hyperobjects: Philosophy and Ecology after the End of the World* (Minnesota: University of Minnesota Press, 2013), 81.

20 Ibid, 55.

21 Ibid, 82.

22 Ibid, 101.

23 Scott, *Seeing Like a State.*

24 George G. Waldbusser, et al., "Saturation-state Sensitivity of Marine Bivalve Larvae to Ocean Acidification," *Nature Climate Change* 5, no. 3 (2015): 273; Ashley Dawson, *Extreme Cities: The Peril and Promise of Urban Life in the Age of Climate Change* (New York: Verso Books, 2017).

than it can be removed from the realms of economy and environment. As actors in a constructed world, we might accept that, like a hyperobject, reality itself is not legible, but rather an intertwining of narratives – glimpses into the components which construct our world. Acknowledging that the "common world has still to be collected and composed,"[35] we need access to other ways of knowing that light up other connections in the mesh where we are acting.

Disciplinary boundaries exist for myriad technical, historical, and cultural reasons, and the ensuing epistemologies allow us to understand reality in a variety of rich and specific ways. Embracing multidisciplinarity is, by definition, based on an acceptance of the existence of discrete disciplines, each with a distinct way of organizing reality. Multidisciplinarity reflects a "YES, AND" attitude to composing the world: YES, designers have specific and technical tools with which to interpret the world; AND designers absorb other narratives they couldn't or wouldn't typically access. While disciplinary silos amputate alternative compositions of reality, expanding and overlapping disciplinary boundaries can allow us access to alternative narratives. To understand the ripples proliferated by any object, the teams that create them need to be both multidisciplinary and multi-epistemological: embodying multiple ways of seeing and interpreting the world.

What happens to this embrace of intertwining narratives in the context of the real economic and cultural constraints within which most designers must operate, where they are rarely even invited into critical, high-level strategic meetings? We would suggest that a reframing of the practice of design needs to start in the way that designers are educated. Rather than focusing primarily on technical or highly discipline-specific skills, a design education could embrace, from the outset, designing as act of curated assemblage as well as creativity. Rather than delineating a hard edge around the design project–the building, the park, the urban district to be redeveloped–designers and students might add a Gaussian blur to that line, incorporating the design object's interobjective mesh, engaging multiple narratives and impacts. When the terms used to talk about design are expanded to include additional epistemologies, students understand how a design project relates to complex systems and reinforces or breaks down existing power structures. In addition to enabling richer projects, the ability to see things from various perspectives is strategic: if designers are to operate as key decision-makers in complex projects, they need to be able to both communicate in the language of the non-designer and identify opportunities for action within larger systems.

This metaphysical methodology would also require new forms of representation: new ways of capturing the fluid, interconnected network in which we operate. Our tools can also predefine the perimeters and parameters of our work. Our 2- and 3-D digital representation tools fail to represent dynamic environmental contexts or "the continuous demands of so many conflicting stakeholders –users, communities of neighbors, preservationists, clients, representatives of the government and city authorities."[36] New tools for understanding and communicating projects might too borrow from other fields: actor-network diagrams, narratives, software programs, performance artwork.

We are inculcated, from the first day of design school, into a specific disciplinary culture that aims to impress upon students a particular way of seeing the world. The impact of this experience is immeasurable, and often lifelong: we define ourselves as landscape architects, or as architects, or as urban designers, in part by drawing a line and separating ourselves from what we are not. But, as Latour and Morton have shown us, the world doesn't care about our lines: it is full of things, hyperobjects, interobjective meshes, hidden connections, infinite narratives. To see past the blinders of our professions and remain relevant, we need a different kind of conceptual framework for action. Our lines need more blur.

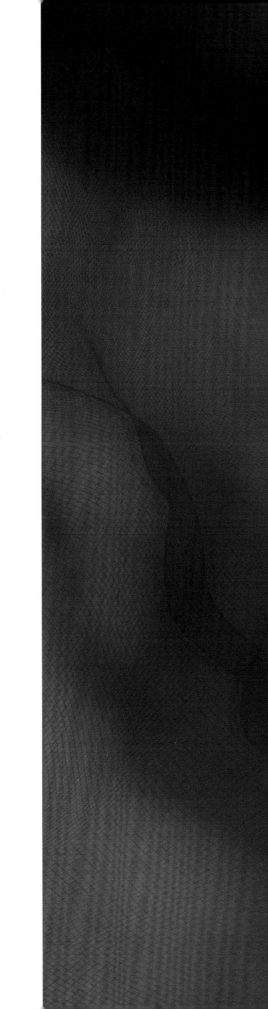

25 Billy Fleming, "Rebuild by Design in New York City: Investigating the Competition Process and Discussing its Outcomes," *Ri-Vista* 15, no. 2 (2017): 200–15.

26 Dawson, *Extreme Cities*.

27 Greet De Blok, "Ecological Infrastructure in a Critical-Historical Perspective: From Engineering 'Social' Territory to Encoding 'Natural' Topography," *Environment and Planning A* 48, no. 2 (2016): 382.

28 Kate Aranoff, "Puerto Rico is on Track for Historic Debt Forgiveness," https://theintercept.com/2017/10/04/puerto-rico-debt-forgiveness-hurricane-maria/ (accessed February 26, 2018).

29 See, 1984 United States Code Chapter 9, Title 11.

30 Umair Irfan, "Puerto Rico is starting to Take Solar Power More Seriously," https://www.vox.com/energy-and-environment/2017/10/19/16431312/elon-musk-richard-branson-clean-energy-puerto-rico-solar-batteries-microgrid (accessed February 26, 2018).

31 Term coined by Zygmunt Bauman. See, Harald Welzer, *Climate Wars: What People Will be Killed for in the 21st Century* (London: Polity, 2012).

32 US Census Bureau, https://www.census.gov/quickfacts/PR (accessed February 26, 2018).

33 The Coastal Marine Resource Center, http://resilientpowerpr.org/resilientpr/ (accessed February 26, 2018).

34 Reinhold Martin, "Financial Imaginaries: Toward a Philosophy of the City," *Grey Room* 42 (2011): 60–79.

35 Latour, *Reassembling the Social*, 118.

36 Morton, *Hyperobjects*, 70.

Andrés Jaque is founder and director of the Office for Political Innovation (Madrid and New York), and associate professor and director of the Master of Science program in Advanced Architectural Design at the Columbia University Graduate School of Architecture, Planning, and Preservation. His practice develops architectural projects that bring inclusivity into daily life. Through built works, performances, and exhibitions, his work instigates crucial debates for contemporary architecture. Recently, his research has explored dating apps and the role these technologies play in society. Colin Curley caught up with Andrés in New York on behalf of LA+ Journal.

+ Your design work encompasses a spectrum of architecture interiors, film, exhibit design, teaching, and performance. How do these different methods of design exploration and production work together within your practice?

It's a very good question. The reason my practice is so diversified is because reality is diversified. So, in order to gain an agency and be relevant to architecture, I ended up doing many different things and connecting them. This is something that has two directions for me. One is towards the future: how I will reinvent daily life, society, and the world we live by (and I would say *by*, rather than *in*). That means that we have to reinvent space, but also connections, infrastructures, and performances and the way we understand them.

It also works backwards. By connecting all these different practices, we also can look back to our built architecture and realize that we could never really understand buildings without looking at the way they were used, the way they would perform, the way they were discussed, and the way things that happen at different scales came together through architecture. For me it's been an adventure that was meant to help me gain an agency in the reinvention of daily life, but also helped me understand much better what architecture is about, and what it's been about.

+ That's a good segue into what you explore through your practice. As the name of your practice, Office for Political Innovation, suggests, your work explores the broader social, societal, and political dimensions of architecture and the built environment. How do you define the politics of architecture within your practice, and engage them or work with them through your projects?

Often, we hear that architecture is about providing boxes or containers in which society can be accommodated. I'm totally against this notion because I believe architecture is a part of society, never a neutral container for it. It mediates between actors that are very different – for instance, between mountains or the atmosphere, and people, animals, or machines. What brings them together is architecture.

So, I believe architecture is a mediator that is never just neutral, but connects things with distinct qualities. We can define those qualities as political because they help define what gets connected and what remains disconnected, and because the act of mediation can only be described through terms like "alliance," "sponsorship," "association," "confrontation," and "dispute." All these terms belong to the realm of politics.

But the politics I'm interested in are not the politics of political parties or spoken words. I'm interested in the politics that can be done through material devices or through performances: through design, in general terms. For instance, when we design a ramp, we make it possible for people with wheelchairs to access a location and participate in events that would otherwise be inaccessible. Those are the kinds of politics that I'm interested in: the ones that are done through ramps, through doors, through walls, through structures, through services, pipes, and lights. And that's precisely what I would call material politics, or design politics. In the long run, these politics often gain much more importance than those of spoken words, and that's why I think architecture is very exciting now – precisely because it's political, but can be political in a very particular way.

+ You refer to many of your built projects as devices. Do you consider them to be actors more than objects?

For me, it's important to understand that whatever we do, the objects we produce, the situations we help facilitate are kinds of artifacts. They're not neutral components, but are loaded with agency. That's why I think that we have to find the right terminology to talk about that, and I think the terms "device" and "artifact" are ones that we can all understand, and through which we gain a certain level of capacity to transform things. I would say that it also brings to common ground things that initially could be seen as very different.

For me, for instance, the cell phone is not that different from a building, a big piece of land, or a fracking well. It's a kind of architecture, and we have to find words that enable us to include them in the same conversation. For instance, the conversion of heating systems in New York City from oil to gas was immediately related to the emergence of fracking in areas very close to New York State. In the Susquehanna Valley of Pennsylvania, for example, the heating systems in homes are not independent from the drilling wells. We have to find a way of thinking about architecture that makes it possible to understand many different things as part of the same reality.

+ On the topic of the role of technology in society, in a previous interview, you stated that technology is not only technological devices, but how society is reconstructed by the insertion of those devices. With that in mind, could you expand on how you approach technology, both in critical and practical terms, within your practice?

I can tell you about a project that we did that is quite small, but is probably the largest one that we've done in political terms. It's a project called Escaravox and it's just a pair of shading devices. We can put the two of them in a truck and move them around, but when they deploy they are shading devices that are equipped with speakers, computers, projectors, and lighting systems. They're made available for people to use freely, and typically have more than 500 users every night. People gather around them and spend the night there, playing music, showing photographs to their friends, and organizing lectures. During the day, there is one university that organizes master classes there.

These devices are not very much about material mobilization. They're actually very small in terms of their materiality, but they're huge in their capacity to mobilize society. For me, this is very important. I could say that the architecture I'm interested in is hairy architecture – architecture that has hairs that connect it with other things. When you look at architecture in this way, then you see that the relational dimension is much more expansive than what most buildings get to mobilize, and I think this is crucial.

When we think, for instance, of the architectures that are shaping contemporary life, often they are architectures that even become invisible. For instance, we've been studying Grindr and other hookup apps for a long time. The technology, the servers, and the team that are running Grindr are quite tiny. There are only 92 people for something that is used in almost every country in the world. And Grindr has around 10 million users, so it's actually the size of a country, but it's something that you can fit in a volleyball court. A volleyball court has transformed the way many people relate to each other in the world, all around the world.

I think we need to readjust what it is that we consider scale in architecture. I think that the architectures that are most relevant now are interscalar, in that they decouple their material investment from the social mobilization they are able to initiate.

Opposite: Escaravox, Madrid (2012).

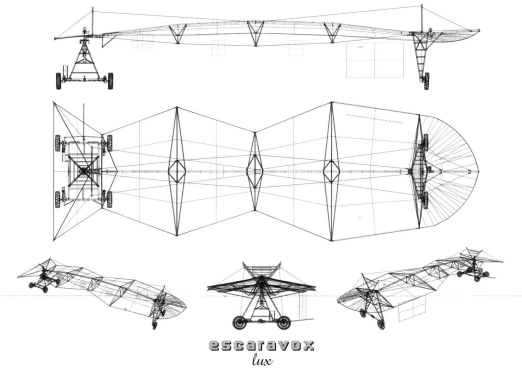

escaravox
lux

+ I'd like to discuss a little bit more about the research that you've been doing on dating apps and online social networks through Intimate Strangers and Pornified Homes. I'm curious to know how, as an architect, you were drawn to that line of inquiry in terms of looking at the technology itself?

What I've learned is that architecture never happens alone, and it's very important to find ways to design heterogeneous constellations of architectures. I will give you an example. If you look at the way people meet in a romantic way now, discos and clubs are no longer that important. When you look at places like the Meatpacking District, that in the '80s was at the very heart of the nightlife in New York City, it's no longer possible to see the same scenarios of social interaction that were once very easy to spot.

What is happening now takes place in the combination of cell phones with apartments, because, nevertheless, Chelsea is one of the world's favorite locations for Grindr users to switch on their apps. Why? Because the apartment towers and the High Line became kind of a desirable and very aspirational location. And the combination of these different architectures is mobilized through Grindr as a possibility for people to satisfy the desire to meet someone.

What is interesting for me is that we can learn from that. What can public space—collective space for interaction, the space for urbanity—learn from the possibility of combining and articulating different technologies to produce what in the past could be done just with space, or mostly with space? I believe the future of architecture will be in the way all these different technologies (and by technology I mean apartments, buildings, parks, and streets as much as home computers and laptops) can be articulated from design.

So, I think the next design—the design that will gain relevance or that will bring architecture into relevance—is probably the one that mediates heterogeneous technologies. And the problem is that we're not ready for that, so we need to transform our training, transform our tools, and define for ourselves new ways of working and even new ways of engaging in society. We need to seek new possibilities for clients to make ourselves more visible. And that is the challenge that, in a way, we all share.

SHOULD THE PLANET BE A DESIGN PROJECT?

IF MARS IS THE ANSWER, WHAT IS THE QUESTION?

CATLI

+ That relates to the idea that designers today need to be expert generalists: we need to know a little bit about everything to do one thing well. I'm curious to know if you agree with that, and what you believe are the essential skills for designers to critically engage this ever-evolving landscape of technology.

Opposite: Still from Pornified Homes (2016).
Above: Rendering of The Future Starts Here exhibition (2018).

I think there are two questions here. The first one I would respond to by saying that architects are no longer solo creators. We are understanding that we have to work in networks of different professionals and different knowledges. Multidisciplinarity and transdisciplinarity are not options now. Relevance only happens when people with different knowledges get together, and that is something that is already reshaping the way we understand architectural design practices.

The second question I think is equally relevant, and it's about scale. I believe that we have to go beyond the distribution of scales to specialties in architectural practices. We're used to thinking that architecture needs different people to deal with the finer scale of industrial design, interior design, and furniture design. Then we have architects dealing with buildings, architect-engineers dealing with big buildings and skyscrapers, and urban designers to deal with the scale of a district. We have urbanists who deal with planning, and we even have territorial planners.

I think this practice of segregating by scales is very counterproductive. The challenge now is to find ways to develop practices that can be trans-scalar – that can operate at the tiny scale of a table, or even smaller, and do it in a way that a big change can be produced at the scale of the environment. Equally, when we are operating in the environment, we probably want to test what is happening at the small scale.

You can think, for instance, of Equinox, because Equinox designs the bodies of people as much as it is becoming a real estate agency bringing huge transformations to parts of cities and contributing to gentrification. At the same time, they develop a transnational network of interventions that end up having a scale that no city could reach. So I think that when we look at things like Equinox, we can understand that architecture can gain agency, but operate in between and across different scales.

+ Along those lines, you mentioned earlier Chelsea being the world's favorite location for Grindr users. Do you think that there are lessons to be learned for designers of future cities from the research that you've done on dating apps in terms of how we occupy cities and public spaces?

Yes. I think we perceive an appetite to rethink the role architecture can play in turning our daily life political. And by that, I mean that many of us are feeling that civil society is being threatened – that it's been impoverished in the last years. The historical role of architecture to empower the polis and to think of urbanity as the origin of citizenship, I think, is at stake.

Architects have an opportunity to consider our traditions and think about how we can make them current. What is the update that we need to become relevant? What I've seen from my research is that most of the innovations in human and non-human interaction have been developed on the side of individual interests, and I think there's a great need to rethink those innovations and even invent new ones that can turn things collective, and help produce civil society.

+ So, given the diversity of your research and built work, how do you define success as a designer?

I find success in the capacity of architecture to empower the valuable alternative. I will give you an example. In the last years, the infrastructures that deal with wastewater in New York have been totally centralized and black-boxed. They have been made inaccessible, and even imperceptible, making people think that waste can disappear, when what happens is that is sent to other places that have less capacity to make decisions about their environmental quality. This segregation of toxicity is a way of producing inequality.

So, by looking at the way wastewater is dealt with in a place like New York, we can see what is happening to rising rents and the disappearance of low-income people in the city. When we did the installation Cosmo for the MoMA PS1 Young Architect's Program, we were trying to bring an alternative to that, using the huge visibility of the PS1 to raise an issue. We can think of toxicity in different terms. We can design cohabitation with toxicity and by doing that we can have a say in the way our societies are dealing with inequality. If we could reimagine New York City as a place where toxicity can be dealt with here, then I think we can probably find a better society happening, a much more exciting one, and in the long run, even one that has a much stronger, resilient economy.

So architecture is a little bit of a David versus Goliath, with the capacity to present alternatives. Alternatives have a very unexpected trajectory and I'm sure that within a few years, the discussion in New York will be how to bring back the toxicity. When we track this, there will be a number of initiatives, and maybe Cosmo is one of them, that will come from the realm of architecture.

+ On the topic of technology and the future, you've recently been involved in The Future Starts Here exhibition at the Victoria and Albert Museum in London. What can you tell us about that exhibition?

I'm particularly excited to work on this exhibition because it is part of the V&A's tradition of discovering the design of our environments by understanding how society is constructed. The way people dress, their rooms, their highways, are crucial in understanding what possibilities they find as citizens to connect with other things and to engage with others.

The second thing I'm happy with is that the exhibition presented a big design challenge. How do you render things that are so ordinary, or how do you render the tensions that are embodied in ordinary situations, in a way that they become visible and easy to discuss by people who are used to seeing them without paying much attention? I think this challenge has been a great opportunity for us to grow and to learn a lot about the way design plays a key role in the making of what is possible and what is likely to be possible.

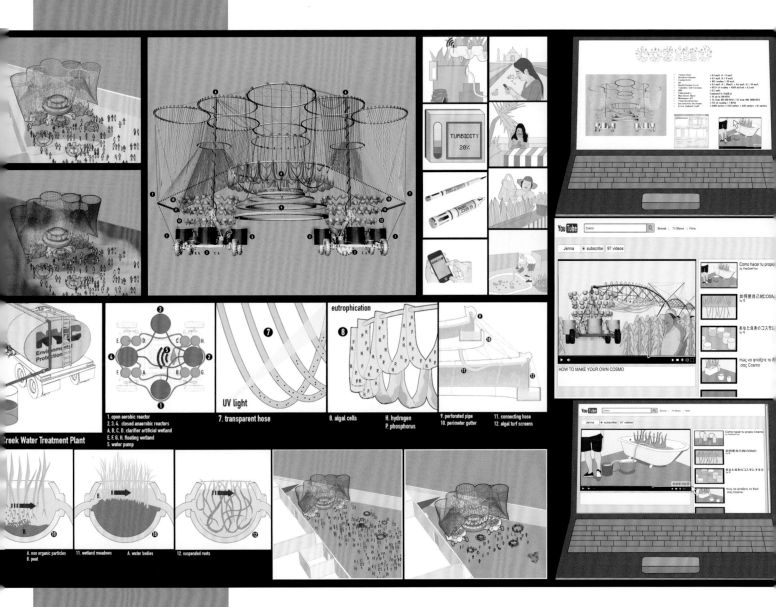

Above: Cosmo (2015).

+ Based on that experience, are you optimistic about the future in terms of what design can do to address some of the challenges we face in society today?

I feel we're probably in a post-optimism situation. We have evidence that there are many things going wrong now that we cannot stop. We have to use our capacities to change things and also to understand that what we do has a great capacity to present alternatives, and to reinvent what happens around us. I'm trying to work forward from the question of whether we're optimistic or pessimistic to see what it is we can do to change things. And there's a lot we can do. I think that, in a way, brings an energy and a feeling of connection with others that also creates momentum; and I think that momentum is a good current alternative to optimism.

PERSPECTIVES ON BEAUTY

THOMAS JACOBSEN

Thomas Jacobsen is a professor of experimental and biological psychology at Helmut Schmidt University, Hamburg, Germany. He holds a PhD from the Max Planck Institute of Cognitive Neuroscience and is author of over 100 journal publications and two monographs in the area of neurocognitive psychology, including auditory processing, language, empirical aesthetics, and executive function. In 2008, Jacobsen received the Alexander Gottlieb Baumgarten Award of the International Association of Empirical Aesthetics.

+ PSYCHOLOGY, AESTHETICS, DESIGN

Opposite: The seven perspectives of the psychology of aesthetics.

Often we prefer the more beautiful entity to the one that is less so. Great designs can help us feel elevated, or more at one with the world. At times, the beautiful item does not function well, yet still we prefer it. Sometimes preferences seem to be universal, and sometimes we argue a lot. The [neurocognitive] psychology of aesthetics seeks to describe and explain all of these phenomena. Rooted in today's academic psychology and cognitive neuroscience, a wealth of methodological options is at our disposal. In fact, the psychology of aesthetics (or, as it has been termed, experimental aesthetics) is the second-oldest branch of experimental psychology.[1] In 1876 Gustav Theodor Fechner applied experimental techniques to the study of aesthetic appreciation in a psychophysical way, and scholars have pursued this paradigm ever since.

Many determinants of aesthetic experience and behavior have been identified. It has been reported that aesthetic experience and judgments are affected by an object's symmetry or asymmetry, complexity or simplicity, novelty or familiarity, proportion or composition, and protypicality, as well as the semantic content as opposed to formal qualities of design. In addition, many factors are known to influence aesthetic judgments, including aspects of a person's emotional state, education, and historical, cultural or economic background, and the object's appeal to social status or financial interest. Various situational aspects also play a role; for example, we might appreciate the same object differently in a museum compared to a supermarket. In addition, aesthetic judgment is also determined by inter-individual differences. These and other factors illustrate the fact that aesthetic experiences and behavior are subject to a complex network of stimulus-, person-, and situation-related influences.

The psychophysical study of aesthetics can be tested in relation to various areas, which may be best characterized via the seven perspectives shown in the adjacent chart. One perspective starts with the object of aesthetic appreciation: the various domains of aesthetics, like painting, sculpture, opera, theatre, architecture, design, and many more. In contrast to a subjective first-person view, features of the objects are being assessed and characterized. One example is the feature of symmetry, which has long been argued to be an important characteristic of beauty.

In a series of studies since 2002, I and my research partners have employed the symmetry feature in our visual stimuli. Using functional MRI, we investigate the neural correlates of aesthetic judgments of beauty in response to visual stimuli of novel graphic patterns in a trial-by-trial cuing setting using binary responses (symmetric, not symmetric; beautiful, not beautiful).[2] Symmetry, and of course all other features of objects, can be looked at assuming a diachronic

Person
Individual Differences
Group Differences
Expert / Non-Expert
Differences

Situation
Schemata
Scripts

Content
Painting
Sculpture
Music
Literature
Food

Diachronia
Biological Evolution
Cultural Evolution
Fashion
Temporal Stability

PSYCHOLOGY
OF
AESTHETICS

Body
Biology
Neurosciences
Brain

Ipsichronia
Culture
Social Processes
Sub-Culture

Mind
Cognition
Emotion
Attitudes
Prototypes

(development over time), as well as a synchronic (similarities at a point in time) or ipsichronic (differences at a point in time) perspective. Symmetry, in particular, has been argued to be evolutionarily important. Different cultures over time, as well as synchronously, can value symmetry more or less so. One apparent paradox in our research resulted from the fact that in the experimental aesthetics literature, symmetry has frequently been held as a universal for aesthetic preference. Numerous past studies have shown symmetric items to be judged more beautiful, on average, than non-symmetric ones. On the other hand, art history and art generally hold that symmetry is a less important feature. However, a recent empirical study by Leder and colleagues has revealed that both is actually the case.[3] In this study, groups of art experts and non-experts were asked to provide spontaneous beauty ratings of visual stimuli that varied in symmetry and complexity. Art laymen preferred symmetric stimuli over non-symmetric ones, while the opposite was the case for artists and art historians. While for art and design laymen symmetry often is a positive indicator of beauty, individuals nonetheless differ greatly with respect to the degree of using symmetry for their aesthetic judgments of beauty. These inter-individual differences between beholders meant that a sensible group judgment policy could not be derived in a number of studies.

Aesthetic appreciation is always situated. It happens in an interaction of person (e.g., individual/group differences, expert/non-expert), situational context (e.g., natural environment, museum, laboratory), and content or stimulus (e.g., painting, sculpture, music, literature, food). These lead to color preferences being dependent on the context of color use.[4] Preference for a given color differs depending on culturally determined usage in different contexts. While being least preferred as an abstract color patch, a color can well be most preferred for a given design function. Anecdotal examples of context-dependent selection include the choice of building materials on the basis of climate conditions, such as the use of cold material (e.g., concrete or marble) in a hot climate. Another aspect of the situatedness of aesthetic appreciation in empirical aesthetics research pertains to the location of testing participants. Researchers have begun to study aesthetic appreciation outside the laboratory in the field. In order to achieve more ecologically valid settings for experimental aesthetics studies, Wagner and colleagues have produced a theatre performance to investigate the aesthetic enjoyment of the negative emotion of anger,[5] while Hanich and colleagues have taken participants to view sad movies in a cinema to study the state of being emotionally moved.[6]

The multifactorial determination of aesthetic appreciation and production makes for a complex research topic. It can be approached from different vantage points. As mentioned earlier, episodes of aesthetic processing can be investigated as an interaction of situation, person, and content. Each of these perspectives have essential features to contribute, as the above examples illustrate. The cultural sciences, the humanities, and the arts routinely use diachronic and synchronous/ipsichronic perspectives to analyze phenomena in the world of aesthetics. Things evolve over time, whether through biological or technical evolution, and they change more or less arbitrarily with fashion. Comparative and cross-cultural studies of synchronous aesthetics phenomena compliment the diachronic approach.

Combined, these perspectives strive to provide a comprehensive account of all aesthetic practices. Contemporary psychology

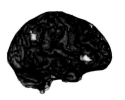
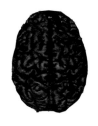
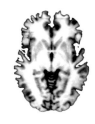

Aesthetic vs Symmetry Judgment

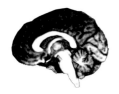

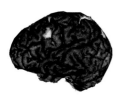

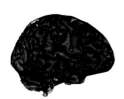

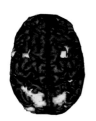

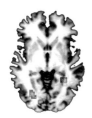

Symmetry vs Aesthetic Judgment

and cognitive neuroscience use the psychophysical mind-brain perspective to investigate mental processing architecture along with its biological underpinnings in a pragmatic dualistic way. Taken together, these seven perspectives make for a framework for the psychology of aesthetics.[7] This is a profoundly interdisciplinary and trans-disciplinary endeavor: while art historians and psychologists investigate the aesthetic preference for symmetry, we also have literary scholars working together with psychologists to unpack the emotional powers of poetry.[8]

As the seven perspectives of my framework for the psychology of aesthetics might indicate, we are bound to identify more instances of aesthetics preference that are being driven by an intricate interplay of both biology and culture. While symmetry has been held to be a universal feature of beauty in many content domains, the example of the cited study shows that culture has the power to turn this preference around. In future research, we will find more striking, seemingly paradoxical effects of nature and nurture on aesthetic appreciation, keeping in mind that these are being implemented in anatomically identical brains of modern man. The future will hopefully see many more joint endeavors of this kind.

1 G.T. Fechner, *Vorschule der Aesthetik* (Leipzig: Breitkopf & Härtel, 1876).

2 Thomas Jacobsen, et al., "Brain Correlates of Aesthetic Judgment of Beauty," *NeuroImage* 29, no. 1 (2006): 276–85; Thomas Jacobsen & Lea Höfel, "Descriptive and Evaluative Judgment Processes: Behavioral and Electrophysiological Indices of Processing Symmetry and Aesthetics," *Cognitive, Affective & Behavioral Neuroscience* 3, no. 4 (2003): 289–99; Thomas Jacobsen & Lea Höfel, "Aesthetic Judgments of Novel Graphic Patterns: Analyses of Individual Judgments," *Perceptual and Motor Skills* 95, no. 3 (2002): 755–66.

3 Helmut Leder, et al., "Symmetry is Not a Universal Law of Beauty," *Empirical Studies of the Arts* (June 13, 2018).

4 Allan Whitfield, "Individual Differences in Evaluation of Architectural Colour: Categorization Effects," *Perceptual and Motor Skills* 59 (1984): 183–86.

5 Valentin Wagner, et al., "Anger Framed: A Field Study on Emotion, Pleasure, and Art," *Psychology of Aesthetics, Creativity, and the Arts* 10, no. 2 (2016): 134–46.

6 Julian Hanich, et al., "Why We Like to Watch Sad Films. The Pleasure of Being Moved in Aesthetic Experiences," *Psychology of Aesthetics, Creativity, and the Arts* 8, no. 2 (2014): 130–43.

7 Thomas Jacobsen, "Bridging the Arts and Sciences: A Framework for the Psychology of Aesthetics," *Leonardo* 39, no. 2 (2006): 155–62.

8 Winfried Menninghaus, et al., "The Emotional and Aesthetic Powers of Parallelistic Diction," *Poetics* 63 (2017): 47–59.

Left: Functional MRI is used to investigate the brain's responses to visual stimuli consisting of novel graphic patterns.

IN CONVERSATION WITH
Anthony Dunne+Fiona Raby

Anthony Dunne + Fiona Raby are, in every possible sense of the word, designers. In the work of their practice, their teaching, and their writing they reframe the way society understands the world around it, offering momentary glimpses into other possible realities. As educators–previously at the Royal College of Art in London and currently at the New School in New York–Dunne + Raby are continuously redefining the role of design in society. Not by imagining better, sleeker, or more efficient "products," but by creating work that is simultaneously curious, provocative, novel, inspiring, and unexpected. These speculations are not driven by industry or the market, but by an interest in alternate realities that might emerge from engaging in, what they term, "social dreaming." **Christopher Marcinkoski** interviewed the designers for *LA+ Journal*.

+ For those unfamiliar with your writing and work, can you briefly describe what you mean by speculative design, and what you see as its primary value(s)? And as a follow-up, how would you differentiate this kind of work from what one might otherwise describe or characterize as art practices?

Speculative design is a living, constantly evolving set of practices rather than a dogma or a theory so we have always resisted trying to define it too precisely. An ex-student of ours, currently working on a PhD exploring speculative design within a Chinese cultural context, told us her supervisor suggested using the term design speculations rather than speculative design – that makes a lot of sense as it shifts the focus back onto the work and specific projects rather than general descriptions or definitions.

With our book *Speculative Everything* (2013), we wanted to open up a space where speculative forms of design practice could thrive alongside more traditional modes of practice. It was intended to offer an alternative design framework for designers who instinctively rejected solution-oriented approaches to design but who struggled to find a context that celebrated criticality, imagination, and materiality. We provided many examples and references for people to begin to assemble their own forms of speculative practice rather than setting out how we

think it should be done. In the years since the book was published, speculative design has been embraced by all sorts of organizations and applied to many different professional, academic, and cultural contexts. As it comes into contact with different issues and challenges it continues to morph and mutate. For us, the most important thing is that imagining alternatives to how things are now gains more acceptance within design, especially in design education. But this does not mean it has to be about futures; in fact, for us, we find futures as the primary way of framing design speculations to be extremely limiting.

This all might sound a bit obvious to architects where there is a history of this kind of work going back hundreds of years, but in design, when it has happened, it has been in the service of marketing. For example, in the automotive industry there is a relatively long tradition of developing concept cars to test new markets and communicate new directions. We have focused on decoupling speculation from this role and making it available for a wider range of more socially oriented uses. We're very conscious of overlaps with architecture, literature, film, and art, but always try to focus on what design speculations can bring to the conversation that complement those of other disciplines.

+ In the first chapter of *Speculative Everything*, you write that much of design is too often oriented towards "fiddling with the world out there, rather than the ideas and attitudes inside our heads that shape the world out there." Does a desire to solve problems foreclose on the possibility of a critical design practice?

Not at all. They are not mutually exclusive. Our argument is against prioritizing problem solving above all else – of seeing everything, no matter how complex, as a problem to be solved. We'd like to see a greater plurality of approaches in design.

+ In reflecting on your work, as well as the various projects included in *Speculative Everything*, it seems quite clear that you do not have a predilection for or fixation with any particular strain of technology, but rather are quite pluralistic about sources of inspiration. Do you see the implications of technology as more central to your work than the technology itself?

Yes, we do, especially when we were leading the Design Interactions program at the Royal College of Art in London. Working within the field of interaction design (very broadly defined), one of our goals was to move beyond using design to develop new applications for technology in an industry setting and instead to explore potential implications and consequences for it in more public settings. Recently, we have begun to focus on the other end of the process – the values and belief systems that drive technological development.

One of the attractions of joining The New School was being able to work with colleagues in disciplines such as anthropology, history, sociology, philosophy, and politics to explore other ways of seeing and understanding the world. In this context, design can serve as a catalyst for interdisciplinary imagining, and once these ideas are brought into a more public context, hopefully, they can spark further imagining. None of our

Previous Page and Opposite: "Foragers: Designs for an Overpopulated Planet" (2009).
Left: "Algae Digester: Designs for an Overpopulated Planet" (2009).

designs are intended to be implemented in any form; their purpose is to enrich and broaden discussions about the kind of world(s) people wish to live in – not in the future, but now. We're very interested in exploring the role design can play in this process.

+ You point out that in much of contemporary design discourse, there is a tension between usefulness and fiction – that fiction is seen as something negative or wasteful. Why is it important that design understands fiction and speculation as means to resist or inflect dominant social mores or intractable economic models?

The process of deciding on what is considered real, and what is not, is where politics and the imagination meet. Politics today is a battle over the imagination, and work that operates on the imagination by either maintaining pre-existing realities, or by challenging them through alternatives that encourage people to question prevailing worldviews becomes political. As Chiara Bottici and Benoît Challand write in *The Politics of Imagination,* "If politics has become a struggle for people's imagination this is, in the first place, due to the fact that such a struggle takes place within human beings and not just among them." Being aware of this as designers is "doing work politically," to borrow and slightly modify Thomas Hirschhorn's phrase; for practitioners, the politics are in the "how," not the "what." In this way, the unreal becomes political in the sense that it can challenge the limits people place on their own imaginations when it comes to thinking about, and questioning, what is possible.

The binary view, which divides the world of ideas, things, and thoughts into real and not real is extremely damaging to the fostering of imagination and its ability to uncover alternatives to how things are now. Especially when the word "unrealistic" often simply means "undesirable" to those in charge, rendering alternative realities impossible for everyone else. Designers need to move beyond this binary approach to dividing up thoughts, ideas, and things. They all exist

"Augmented Digestive System and Tree Processor: Designs for an Overpopulated Planet" [2009].

after all, just in different ways, otherwise it would not even be possible to think them. Design needs more nuanced ways of understanding and talking about this relationship, one that acknowledges that the real and the not real are just two poles on a subtle and rich spectrum.

A big issue for us in design education, at least in the West, is how the idea of reality—and more specifically, what is real and not real—is dealt with. With a few exceptions, at the heart of most current approaches to design pedagogy is a focus on thinking within existing realities whether social, political, economic, or technological, with the result that the ideas, beliefs, and values that have gotten us into many of the challenges we are currently facing are reproduced through design, endlessly. Yet the underlying logic driving the labelling of certain ideals as real and others as unreal is rarely challenged or even questioned, which leads to an ongoing suppression of the design imagination.

Clearly there are certain features of reality that are fixed, at least for the time being (science concerns itself with these), and there are certain unthinkable imaginary objects that can never exist anywhere, or even be thought. But these are the extremes. In between, there is a rich and fascinating space from which unknown realities might one day emerge. Not just things, but also beliefs, values, hopes, ideals, and dreams – the raw material from which new realities can be constructed.

+ I'd like to turn now to a question of aesthetics, and your choices of modes of representation and materiality. In considering your work, I would characterize it as having a kind of techno-simplicity or neutral modernity. You seem to emphasize a smoothness of form, the brightness of color, the plasticity/artificiality of material, and the absence of detail. There is nothing fuzzy or fussy in the work – it is conspicuously precise. Is this simply a personal predilection, a particular aesthetic ideal of the future, or are there other motivations at play?

A bit of all of these. How do you design for unreality, and what should it look like? How should the unreal, parallel, impossible, unknown, and yet-to-exist be represented? And how, in a design, can you simultaneously capture the real and not real? This is where the aesthetic challenge for speculative design lies, in successfully straddling both. To fall on either side is too easy. As designers working outside a strictly commercial context and aiming to engage people with complex ideas, one could argue that similar to film our designs should be about clear communication. But for us, this assumes a simple model of engagement based on transmitting meaning to a passive viewer. We think it is better to engage people through a skillful use of ambiguity, to surprise, and to take a more poetic and subtle approach to interrelationships between the real and the unreal.

Early on, we located our work within an industrial design and interaction design context. The idea was to turn the language of product design on itself so that the objects looked superficially technological and consumer oriented, but on closer inspection didn't quite make sense due to their functions and reason for existing. We recently did a wonderful residency at Pilchuck Glass School and it reminded us how much materiality can bring to a project, something we want to explore more in future projects.

+ I am curious about the role of the "weird" or the "absurd" in speculative design as an idea, and in your work in particular. It seems to me that there is enormous advantage to using spectacle as a means to provoke thought or reframe possible futures. However, there also seems to be a great deal of risk in relying on these qualities as they can be too easily dismissed as one-liners. Where do these qualities fit into your own work?

That's a problem with a lot of poorly executed speculative design, it focuses on the weird above all else. Hopefully in our work we manage to mix things up in more interesting ways. We like using familiar object typologies like vehicles, furniture, domestic products, and so on – objects people understand and can relate to, but transformed in ways that suggest they embody other values to prevailing ones. They usually have simple forms, but always with something that is not quite right, and that's the quality we spend a lot of time trying to achieve – different kinds of wrongness.

Mark Fisher put it very nicely in his book *The Weird and the Eerie:* "I want to argue that the weird is a particular kind of perturbation. It involves a sensation of wrongness: a weird entity or object is so strange that it makes us feel that it should not exist, or at least it should not exist here. Yet if the entity or object is here, then the categories which we have up until now used to make sense of the world cannot be valid. The weird thing is not wrong, after all: it is our conceptions that must be inadequate." This beautifully captures what we see as the value of the weird.

+ In the context of increasing awareness of the interrelationship of things and actions–ecology in its broadest form–could you comment on the role of the systemic in speculative design? Should we understand the prop simply as a means of entry? Or does the object have some value in and of itself?

Both. I can't think of a single object that is not part of a system, whether an ecology, a system of ideas or beliefs, a technological network or infrastructure, or a legal or regulatory framework. When we see the object it is easy to forget all this. Or maybe simply not be aware of it. In our work, we always try to think through the systems our design would be entangled with, but as we are object focused we don't really show that side of the work. It's just part of the narrative we use to generate the work.

It's a very interesting time to be working with objects. Besides the different modes of existence an object can have (from the virtual to the actual), the different categories (such as models, props, prototypes, mock-ups), and all the cultural baggage attached to each, in addition, ideas from speculative realism, object oriented ontology, actor network theory, and hyperobjects provide wonderful new lenses for thinking about objects in new ways.

+ One final question, you write a great deal about designing for how things could be. Where do you see speculative design practices as having the greatest efficacy (engendering social good, changing behavioral patterns, deepening our awareness of the implications of technological regimes, something else)? Perhaps what you describe as "allowing for the production of billions of individual utopias"?

In design, when a project steps away from the here and now, it is automatically relocated to the future, often a possible (realistic) one. But futures, as a narrative framework, can be very limiting. They restrict the imagination through the requirement to link back to the present (which of course they are nearly always some version of) or extensions of current worldviews. We are more interested in starting with alternative worldviews and using design to give them form. They can be in the future, in the past, or in a parallel present, but most importantly for us, they are simply *not here, not now.*

By working with anthropologists, political scientists, and social theorists, design can contribute to the proliferation of multiple worlds existing in the collective imagination, enlarging it to provide a richer conceptual space from which to uncover alternatives to the present and consider the kind of world(s) people wish to live in. A form of interdisciplinary imagining that aims to inspire further imagining, rather than communicating a vision of how things will or should be. In this role, the designer's task is to give form to a multiverse of hidden possibilities that can contribute to a culture of imaginative alterity materialized in ways that engage the mind by challenging it, shifting its focus, arresting it, motivating, and inspiring. Raising awareness that if reality is not given but made, then it can be unmade, and remade. This is not simply about the reimagining of everyday life—there are plenty of examples of this—it is about using unreality to question the authority of a specific reality in order to foreground its assumptions and ideology.

This is something we are currently exploring in a project we've called the "Many Worlds Working Group." The project began as a series of design responses to conversations about research in history, anthropology, sociology, philosophy, and politics. A colleague described it as a sort of "other world's fair," which we both like. It's a proposal for a new kind of facility for public imagining, set in an alternative Floyd Bennett Airfield on the edge of New York which aims to provide a counterpoint to future visions as the primary framing device for imagining new realities. A sort of anti-futures facility, it would be a place where new worldviews can be developed and formulated into propositions, questions, hypothesis, ideas, and what-ifs – useful fictions materialized through large scale partial prototypes and models forming temporary landscapes of (social) thought experiments made physical.

It is not a place for testing ideas intended to be implemented, nor a public consultation forum, but rather a place where, in response to the complex fusion of politics and technology shaping today's social realities, speculative forms of material culture can be used to provoke new ideas and collective imagining about the kinds of worlds people wish to live in. One of the aims of the project is to experiment with and deepen understanding of the mechanics of unreality – utopias, dystopias, and heterotopias; what ifs and as ifs; hypotheses, thought experiments, and *reductio ad absurdum*; counterfactuals and uchronia, and so on. Synthesizing ideas from political science, anthropology, sociology, history, economics, and philosophy into new worldviews made tangible through an expanded form of design practice. The proposal itself is a question about the nature of futures and how they take shape within a society.

"Huggable Atomic Mushroom: Designs for Fragile Personalities in Anxious Times Project" (2004).

Keith M. Murphy

LETTERING THE LAND

THE SOCIAL WORLD AS
PATTERN/ED LANGUAGE

Keith M. Murphy is associate professor of anthropology at the University of California, Irvine. He has conducted ethnographic research with architects in Los Angeles and furniture designers in Sweden, and is currently researching the cultural and political sides of typography in the United States. He is author of *Swedish Design: An Ethnography* (2015).

✚ ANTHROPOLOGY, DESIGN

It took a while, but anthropologists have at last discovered design. Since anthropology first emerged as the scholarly study of human beings in the late 19th century, many design-adjacent cultural forms like art, craft, and the built environment have featured prominently in the discipline's research portfolio, but the "designed-ness" of these cultural forms has been mostly ignored. Instead, the surface meanings of those cultural forms have simply been *read*: art as reflecting social values, craft as demonstrating a mode of production, and built environments as offering local adaptations to various natural conditions. Of course cultural forms like these, or of all kinds really, don't arise *ex nihilo*. They are *made*, significantly from the effort of human hands, minds, and voices, and it is this making, including designing and its potential complexities, that anthropologists have recently begun to explore more deeply.

Anthropological Designs

Most current understandings of design tend to treat designers as, to borrow Susan Sontag's description of Swedish aesthetes, "pedants of the object,"[1] that is, focused squarely on the details of the particular things they make, including what those things look like and how they work. This characterization is, undoubtedly, quite right in most instances. By comparison, an anthropological approach to design situates that object pedantry—and by "object" I mean, broadly, anything that's designed for some purpose—in a much wider and more nuanced social context, and tries to explain not only how single objects, but also how entire assemblages of designed things come to compose what we experience as the everyday world. Put differently, anthropology offers a relational mode of analysis, a mode of understanding humans and things that foregrounds connections between the social world's basic building blocks, be they of material, ideological, spatial, emotional, linguistic, or natural essences, without necessarily privileging one over the other. If we apply that approach to understanding design, we can say that while design practice does indeed entail the intentional manipulation of order and form in the traditional sense, it also involves working, arranging and distributing other matters (social orders and cultural forms), even in ways that extend beyond designers' own pedantry of their objects.

To explain more fully what I mean by this claim, I want to examine some links between two phenomena, typography and landscape, each with its own designed features and each of which is a significant component of the everyday world. Before getting there, though, I'd like to say a bit more about what I mean by form.

Giving Form

A common aphorism applied to design (and in some languages, like Swedish, it's a true synonym for the term) is "form-giving." Typically form-giving is associated with physical or spatial forms—geometries, sizes, colors, and orders—and designers are treated as "giving" these forms "to" the specific objects they create. Anthropology, too, is concerned with form, but in a much looser sense of the term. Basically, anything that holds a structure or configuration that's recognizable and meaningful to members of some social group can count as a cultural form. A form can indeed be physical, like the shape of a certain architectural feature, or geometrical, like the symbol of the cross in Christianity, but it could also be a form of motion, like the moves of a particular ceremonial dance, or a form of habitation, like how gendered bodies are expected to occupy public space.

What's critical for seeing design anthropologically is understanding how material, physical, and spatial forms meaningfully relate to, and help produce and cultivate, other kinds of cultural forms that collectively constitute the social world, even in cases that designers themselves don't anticipate. Some of these relations are obvious, like how the distributions of walkways in a park produce forms of movement, and the placement of large shade trees alongside those walkways can provide zones of respite from the sun's heat. Or how hostile design features, like skatestoppers and slanted public benches, are placed to prevent certain kinds of people from occupying certain kinds of spaces, thereby producing particular "good" and "bad" forms of inhabiting space (and also, "moral" and "not moral" kinds of people). But many of the forms brought forth by design are both more subtle and more complex, including forms of action and interaction, forms of discourse, forms of thought, and forms of social organization. This perspective requires attending to a much wider variety of forms than is typically associated with design, and also taking them seriously *as forms*, that is, as organized, consistently (if not uniformly) shaped, and regular.

Perhaps another way to think about this is through the lens of a pattern language. In *A Pattern Language: Towns, Buildings, Construction*, Christopher Alexander and colleagues present and elaborate a "language" of titled and numbered entities, or patterns, that when used in combination both identify and offer solutions to a range of problems often experienced in the everyday world.[2] What's critical to this list is that the constitutive elements are, like the forms I've identified above, not all of the same nature. Some of the patterns are structural, like (17) Ring Roads, (21) Four-Story Limit, and (50) T Junctions. Others are more cultural, like (24) Sacred Sites, (58) Carnival, and (66) Holy Ground. Many explicitly concern social organization, like (36) Degrees of Publicness, (75) The Family, and (84) Teenage Society, while others are more focused on actions and interactions, like (63) Dancing in the Streets, (68) Connected Play, and (94)

Sleeping in Public. Several, like (40) Old People Everywhere and (79) Your Own Home, reflect a complex combination of types. What's more, these patterns are scaled from very large, like (2) Distribution of Towns and (42) Industrial Ribbons, to very small, like (65) Birth Places and (74) Animals, and differently specified, from the mostly vague, like (9) Scattered Work and (10) Magic of the City, to very particular, like (20) Mini-Buses and (22) Nine Percent Parking.

For Alexander and his colleagues, this pattern language, a flexible network of sequentially linked forms, was primarily useful as a customizable tool to help designers puzzle through their own individual projects. However, because these patterns were originally derived from careful observation of the lived world, and because the language was assembled agnostically with regard to the "kind" and "nature" of the language's constituent forms, the tool these architects came up with unexpectedly works as a sort of model for understanding design from an anthropological point of view.

Lettering the Land

Anthropologists have spent a lot of time studying how different groups of people interact with and give meaning to the landscapes they inhabit. Dwelling in and moving through space are of course significant modes of interaction with the land, but what anthropologists have long argued is that doing so is never neutral, and always mediated through the experience of cultural forms (like religious beliefs, gender norms, kinship), such that human relations with their environments are largely created and maintained though different webs of meaning. One of the most significant cultural forms that mediates people's relationships with landscape is language, especially in its graphic guise, typography.

Probably the most obvious form that typography takes in urban public space, in a place like Los Angeles,[3] for example, is in signage of different types. There are signs that mark businesses, with a name and a logo, and municipal signs that accomplish proxy-governmental functions, like officially designating a neighborhood, regulating speed, or establishing a particular agency's jurisdiction. There are posters, billboards, and banners advertising events and services that aren't necessarily linked to the space itself, but that might appeal to those who move through it. And on these different signs, or some of them at least, are different languages, signaling different sorts of things, though what's signaled depends on the language. Maybe it's that many speakers of a language live in the neighborhood, or have historically lived in the neighborhood, like the presence of Japanese in LA's Little Tokyo, or maybe certain languages, like French in a restaurant's name, bring some kind of prestige or cachet.

But it's not just the presence of shop signs and street signs that matter for language-ing the urban landscape. There are other forms, too, like spray-painted graffiti, clusters of stickering, and letters and numbers stamped into sidewalk concrete. Language is also placed and positioned in meaningful ways, on billboards high in the sky, signs mounted near the top of a storefront, or maybe closer to eye level on a shop door, or even on sandwich boards close to the ground. And all of those language specimens assume some meaningful style. Some forms look "corporate" and "professional" while others look "small business" and "informal," while still others feel "municipal" or "bureaucratic," all of which may inform how people act in and around them.

To bring this back to form-giving, one way to understand the "linguistic landscape"[4] of a city is as the accumulation of different designed and spatially aligned forms that collectively establish certain conditions for people to take meaning from, and simply live in, urban space. Any given language specimen on the street is connected to a network of designed forms. Take, for example, a restaurant sign, which would connect up with the design of the building, its interior design, the restaurant logo, the sign's physical shape, size, and color, and of course the typeface in which the restaurant's name is written. Each of these involves a professional designer giving form to their specific projects, all pedants of their particular objects; but when combined with other innumerable projects—other businesses, other signs, other advertisements and banners—a whole typographic ecology begins to take shape.

Letterforms can say a lot about a place, but they can also produce and project other social and cultural forms within a linguistic landscape. For instance, the relative density of language on shop signs typically corresponds to levels of gentrification in a neighborhood—where more words mark a traditional neighborhood small business, and fewer words mark more gentrification—and certainly to people's everyday perceptions of what "kinds" of people can or should occupy urban space.[5] But it's not just the density of words that matter. The kind and diversity of language and typography matter, too. Along Western Avenue in Koreatown, Los Angeles, the visual environment is cluttered with different kinds of signs, languages,

and alphabets. Moving down the avenue, it's common to see three languages (Korean, Spanish, and English) represented on shop signs and advertisements. Two scripts are commonly used (Roman for English and Spanish, and Hangul for Korean), but in both scripts the most common typefaces are drawn with blunt, sans serif letterforms, rather than stylized serif fonts or hanja stylizations (a way of writing Korean that makes it look more like Chinese characters). And there is often seemingly little attention paid to the overall arrangement of these specimens, as each business, each advertiser, and each sign-maker is focused on a single task, rather than the general look or feel of the place.

Note that this isn't the same thing as the use of "ethnically-themed" typography, which is usually intended to brand a shop or even an entire area as "authentic," despite its rarely being so.[6] Common examples like "Latino," "Asian," and "Irish" typefaces are all meant to invoke a particular sense of foreignness, though usually of a familiar sort. The forms these typefaces take both rely on and reproduce stereotypes about the ethnic or racial groups they're associated with, even though the fonts may not be commonly used among the groups they're referencing. But when there is an abundance of certain typography on the landscape, like the proliferation of Hangul in Koreatown, the typeface graphically casts a shared public identity of the people who live in the neighborhood.

If you travel a few miles north and west from Koreatown to the Melrose Avenue shopping district, things look and feel quite a bit different. Where letterforms are present in public space, they are glaringly *contained* on the landscape, and arranged in a minimalist fashion. The dominant script is Roman. Many shops have single-word names, and those names are self-consciously stylized in a variety of typefaces and boxed within single-color fields. Where there is stickering or graffiti, it appears controlled and intentional, rather than opportunistic and inimical to more "official" graphic forms. Melrose is currently a district with no ethnic identities attached to it, though it is often characterized as a white public space, one that is not so much gentrified as explicitly *classed*, although with that comes the same low density of visible language associated with gentrification. This is also clearly a monolingual space, lacking even "ethnically-themed" typography. Like the typographic ecology in Koreatown—although with very different results—this linguistic landscape both projects and invokes a particular kind of social world, one that is raced and classed in particular ways, that invites inhabiting the space in particular ways, and reflects particular forms of social status.

And while its individual elements have been professionally designed, the cultural force of the typographic ecology comes from its overall collective form, and the other forms, the other patterns, it aligns with in creating a social world.

The Moral

One of the key consequences of examining design anthropologically is nudging it out of its object pedantry mode and into a frame that foregrounds the inherent embeddedness of design objects among an assemblage of physical, spatial, and cultural forms. There's a certain symmetry between this perspective and Alexander's notion of pattern language, though less as a tool for practicing design than as a way of understanding how humans live in the world – of which design is just one, though a significant, aspect. Humans will always labor to bring cultural forms together in meaningful patterns, but design is one of the few arenas of human life dedicated to deliberating that process in its finest details. Designers may not have control over everything, but that's okay, since people have a way of working and reworking the world around them every chance they get.

1 Susan Sontag, "A Letter from Sweden," *Ramparts* 8, no. 1 (1969): 23–38, 34.

2 Christopher Alexander et al., *A Pattern Language: Towns, Buildings, Construction* (New York: Oxford University Press, 1977).

3 This analysis is partly inspired by Doug Suisman, *Los Angeles Boulevard: Eight X-Rays of the Body Public*, 25th Anniversary Edition, (Novato, CA: ORO Editions, 2014). In the book, Suisman explores the development and significance of LA's network of boulevards and avenues through a number of mostly body-based metaphors. I am, instead using the metaphor of "ecology."

4 For more on "linguistic landscapes," see Ron Scollon & Suzie Wong Scollon, *Discourses in Place: Language in the Material World* (New York: Routledge, 2003).

5 Shonna Trinch & Edward Snajder, "What the Signs Say: Gentrification and the Disappearance of Capitalism without Distinction in Brooklyn," *Journal of Sociolinguistics* 20, no. 1 (2016), 1–26.

6 Johana Londoño, "The Latino-ness of Type: Making Design Identities Socially Significant," *Social Semiotics* 25, no. 2 (2015), 142–50.

DANE CARLSON
THE HINTERLANDS

Dane Carlson is a landscape designer based both in the United States and Nepal. His design and research practice, REALMS, operates in landscapes throughout the hinterlands of Nepal. It investigates in and acts at points of emerging change in landscapes made increasingly vulnerable by dramatic shifts. Carlson utilizes the methodologies of design anthropology, acting as design catalyst in partnership with communities.

✚ DESIGN ANTHROPOLOGY, LANDSCAPE ARCHITECTURE

Global hinterlands are a vital new frontier for landscape architecture. But as contemporary practice expands across diverse frontiers, the established disciplinary canon is rendered insufficient. For an expanded foundation, the discipline can look to the human history of vernacular adaptation in the landscape, largely overlooked or written out of landscape architecture's exclusive history. Drawing on the work of my design and research practice REALMS, I propose a theory and practice of landscape architecture built on this foundation, driven by the agency and knowledge of people, shaped through collaborative processes, working within systems of movement, making, and worship. This practice rejects simple romantic veneration of the vernacular, asking instead how these place-specific practices can evolve in response to the ubiquitous reach of global capital and culture.

In Theory: An Expanded Foundation

Across global hinterlands, living vernacular landscapes are inseparable from sacred meaning and cultural memory. The lives that define them are drawn from the land, founded on deep histories of embodied knowledge and meaning. They are not nonmodern or premodern, but meld centuries of continuity with emerging change. In places such as the Nepali Himalaya, these landscapes actively demonstrate the complexities of adaptation, the humanity of resiliency, and the agency of memory and meaning.

But they are increasingly subject to vulnerability. Intimate relationships with the resources of place are rendered inadequate by mass outmigration and climate change. Many of these landscapes are no longer peripheral to the state, but at the forefront of exploitative resource extraction and geopolitical maneuvering.[1] New infrastructures that expand mobility and market access accelerate exploitation and exacerbate socio-economic inequality. Though these shifts introduce vulnerability, opportunity lies in hybridity at the intersections of continuity and change. REALMS operates at these intersections; it embraces the fluid humanness of the vernacular

DESIGNING AT THE INTERSECTION OF CONTINUITY AND CHANGE

and a dynamic genius loci as its foundation. It is driven by the methods of design anthropology and engagement with the concrete realities of peoples' daily lives as they respond to emerging change.

The genius loci long embraced by mainstream landscape architecture as a basis for design has proven superficial. It is static, tied by outside observers to aesthetic tradition, metaphysical abstraction, and sweeping cultural generalization. Aesthetic interpretations of place strip the landscape of meaning, denying the generative capacities of people and the processes they initiate, guide, and are subjected to. Marginal populations and systematic inequalities are ignored as cultural practices become lionized monoliths. The "fundamental opposition between universal civilization and autochthonous culture" is a false dichotomy that negates the myriad shades of gray in the human experience between two extremes.[2]

This approach cannot be supported by the established canon of landscape architecture. It is dominated by static, formally designed landscapes fueled by elite patronage in centers of power. As it diverges from this body of precedent, landscape architecture can "emerge from its dependence on the dominant discourses of art and architectural historiography to tell its own story."[3] This is a story of landscape-making as a universally human practice spanning human history from the taming of fire as a landscape-making tool to contemporary design.[4] It is not a history composed of piecemeal landscape traditions and styles, but a continuum of practice fueled by adaptive capacity,

dynamic response, and meaning-making. It reaches beyond the landscapes of landscape designers to those of herders, hunters, gatherers, and shaman. This continuum of landscape practice is founded in the beauty and fluidity of the vernacular, "identified with local custom, pragmatic adaptation to circumstances, and unpredictable mobility...the image of our common humanity: hard work, stubborn hope, and mutual forbearance striving to be love."[5] This story is an expanded foundational narrative for the global practice of landscape architecture.

Across this continuum, landscape-making is driven both by necessity and meaning. Yi-Fu Tuan describes the agency of meaning through what he terms mythical space: "[it] is a conceptual schema, but it is also a pragmatic space in the sense that within the schema a large number of practical activities, such as the planting and harvesting of crops, are ordered."[6] For example, in the Balinese system of rice paddy cultivation, water temples serve as nodes of religious practice, water distribution, and social organization.[7]

But meaning is not only constructed through cosmological or religious narratives. Geographer Doreen Massey describes human-occupied space as a "pincushion of a million stories."[8] Meaning is woven by this web of stories, inhabiting every stone, field, and tree in the landscape, each shaped, neglected, or perceived as part of a human story. These landscape narratives "organize reality, justify actions, instruct, persuade, even compel people to perform in certain ways."[9] To engage more deeply with meaning and the people who generate it allows us

Microclimate-creating wall infrastructure on the slopes above Batang.

Dzong walls preserve moisture gathered by check dams in seasonal flowlines.

to reject disciplinary tropes such as placemaking, increasingly scrutinized as a colonial practice rarely acting on deep engagement with place.[10] This is to approach the fundamental humanness of landscape.

In Gareth Doherty's *Paradoxes of Green*, chronicling a year of fieldwork in Bahrain, the author suggests that the agency of ethnography is its use "in the design process itself, rather than as a retrospective tool," a shift from description to action.[11] This hybridity of observation and action places us *within* the landscape continuum as active participants. Dori Tunstall's definition of design anthropology demonstrates its rootedness in the human dimension: "an interdisciplinary field that seeks to understand the role of design artifacts and processes in *defining what it means to be human*."[12] Design anthropology provides us with the tools "to engage in the meaning-making practices of everyday life wherein the ordinary, daunting, and exhilarating realities of human experience are 'taken hold of' by men and women in the 'company of their gods.'"[13] By doing so, contemporary landscape architecture can position itself as the next evolution in the continuum of human landscape-making, freed from the confines of an inadequate canon.

REALMS is a practice of seeing and learning founded in the experienced phenomena of place and a deeply personal pursuit of landscape, a fascination for beauty, mystery, and humanity. It revels in material and the depth of materiality. Political ecologist Jessica Barnes describes this depth thus: "the material properties of a thing shape the kinds of apparatus employed to extract, process, transport, and utilize it. In the process, they variously facilitate, inhibit, or disrupt forms of society-environment interaction and set the terrain of political possibilities."[14] These apparatuses are formative ingredients of the "social life" of objects – the processes and meanings that determine the nature of material form. Beauty can undoubtedly

be seen in the materials, colors, and textures of the physical landscape. But the origins of beauty are in depth, in the unfolding experiences of meaning, memory, and knowledge-making.

REALMS begins its operations at the scale of daily minutiae, side-by-side with the people who shape them. The lived experience of watching the flock or threshing the crop is a necessary interface between land, people, and designer. Siting these minutiae within the larger contexts of geopolitics, geography, or materiality–systems beyond the reach of personal relationships–allows the designer to approach them objectively. Design is situated at the points of intersection between these systems and the forms, practices, and meanings of daily life.

In Practice: Nepal – City and Hinterland

The city is not the only future. As populations continue to shift to cities, villages and hinterlands are forgotten, places to be vacated and reclaimed by nature. REALMS proposes these as places in which intimate relationships with land can be maintained, memory and narrative retain agency, food self-sufficiency is attainable, adaptive capacity is built, and new technologies, services, and mobility are made available.

Though urban centers and hinterlands are connected by the networks of worldwide urbanism, the ways in which globe- and region-scale abstraction meet the ground are messy. Different people have different abilities to access resources and information, and maintain vastly different agencies within global networks and exchanges. At the Landscape Architecture Foundation Summit in 2016, it was said: "if you love nature, live in the city."[15] For many, the realities are more complex.

Throughout Nepal, village populations have been devastated by a continuing cycle of out-migration and natural disaster. Increasing numbers of men work abroad as unskilled wage

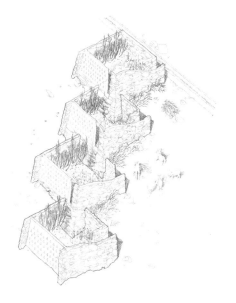

Chhyongkar enclosures within which needed products are grown.

At each rangeland spring, a spring house collects and utilizes precious water.

laborers, mostly in the Middle East, and money sent home dramatically increases family buying power. But many villages are left with few men and broken social structures. Driven by fears of vulnerability and a desire to escape the difficulties of a lifetime tied to the land, many find themselves on equally unsure footing in cities or abroad.[16] As urban populations explode, peoples and places peripheral to state interests remain perpetually neglected or actively marginalized. In the 2015 Gorkha earthquake, over 750,000 homes were destroyed across central Nepal. Two and a half years later, less than 3.5% of those households had received promised reconstruction funding.[17]

New practices, systematized marginalization, and inherited knowledge collide in landscapes across Nepal's Himalayan hinterland. Almost every home in the village of Kerauja remained in ruins 15 months following the Gorkha earthquake due in large part to an ineffectual government reconstruction plan. Disaster response in Kerauja sometimes operates on more localized terms. For example, recent hailstorm was believed to have been brought down on the village by a local deity whose home-tree was being cut down. The cutting was stopped, a shrine was built, and the hailstorm ceased. In the Langtang Valley, semi-nomadic herding remains widespread despite massive disaster-induced loss of life. Mane walls, sacred infrastructures made from stones carved with the Tibetan Buddhist mantra, trace the boundaries of past landslides, rockfalls, and avalanches.[18] These are the landscapes in which REALMS operates.

In the center of Nepal's northern border, the district of Mustang sticks like an upthrust thumb onto the edge of the Tibetan plateau. Mustang is still dominated by lives intimately tied to the land, cyclical change, and pervasive sacred presence. Sacred infrastructures mediate between village boundaries and the realms of deities or serve as memorials to the dead.

Seasonal movements of livestock (goats, sheep, yaks, and the yak/cow hybrid *dzopa*) remain integral to daily life despite being curtailed by a closed border to the north.

But Mustang is increasingly defined by change. Outmigration has left fields and homesteads empty or significantly under-manned as people seek economic opportunity elsewhere. Empty homes are occupied by migrant tenants void of surety or security. Tourism brings new money to a few people in a handful of villages while straining the limited resources of the landscape. Villages have been relocated as their streams disappear. Patterns of ritual regeneration fade. Road construction opens trade routes for cash crop exports, provides access to necessary services, and exacerbates inequality for marginal communities by compounding expense and unreliability while directly benefiting the wealthy.[19]

Flocks of goats, yaks, and sheep are critical to local livelihoods. Flock owners belong to established castes. Shepherds, with rare exception, are semi-itinerant and own no livestock. Flocks are raised in village uplands, largely rainless, increasingly snowless, and continually desiccated by the unrelenting Mustang wind. Shepherds spend eight months or more each year living with their flocks in stone shelters scattered across these rangelands. Available fodder is dwindling: in the spring of 2018 several flocks in Dzong village lost every new kid to starvation. Eagles, leopards, and snow leopards are frequent predators, and conflicts with wildlife conservation persist. Low caste, non-Mustangi shepherds hold little social capital, and a lack of trust is common between owners and *rongba* (lowlander) shepherds.

A series of proposed landscape interventions demonstrates the potential landscape agency of the shepherd. The crux of this proposal is not physical intervention, but positions

1 Vincent Javet, et al., "Landscape as Geopolitics: Beyond Colonial and Capitalist States," *Ground* 40 [2018]: 26.

2 Kenneth Frampton, "Towards a Critical Regionalism: Six Points for an Architecture of Resistance," in Hal Foster [ed.], *The Anti-Aesthetic: Essays on Postmodern Culture* [New York: New Press, 2002].

3 Elizabeth Meyer, "The Expanded Field of Landscape Architecture," in George F. Thompson & Frederick R. Steiner [eds], *Ecological Design and Planning* [New York: John Wiley & Sons, Inc., 1997], 50.

4 Wendy Ashmore & A. Bernard Knapp, *Archaeologies of Landscape: Contemporary Perspectives* [Oxford: Blackwell, 2003], 6.

5 John Brinkerhoff Jackson, *Discovering the Vernacular Landscape* [New Haven: Yale University Press, 2009], vii.

6 Yi-Fu Tuan, *Space and Place: The Perspective of Experience* [Minneapolis: University of Minnesota, 2014], 17.

7 J. Stephen Lansing, *Priests and Programmers: Technologies of Power in the Engineered Landscape of Bali* [Princeton: Princeton University Press], 1991.

8 Social Science Bites, "Doreen Massey on Space," www.socialsciencebites.com [accessed September 10, 2017].

9 Anne Whiston Spirn, *The Language of Landscape* [New Haven: Yale University Press, 2000], 48.

10 Javet, "Landscape as Geopolitics," 25.

11 Gareth Doherty, *Paradoxes of Green: Landscapes of a City-State* [Oakland: University of California Press, 2017], 39.

12 Ibid [emphasis added].

13 Georgina Drew, "Beyond Contradiction: Sacred-Profane Waters and the Dialectics of Everyday Religion," *HIMALAYA, Journal of the Association for Nepal & Himalayan Studies* 36, no. 2, [2016]: 72.

14 Jessica Barnes, *Cultivating the Nile: The Everyday Politics of Water in Egypt* [Durham, NC: Duke University Press, 2014], 29.

15 James Corner, "Landscape City" [paper presented at the Landscape Architecture Foundation Summit, Philadelphia, June 10, 2016].

16 Samantha Day, "The Labor Exit: Shifting Agrarian Livelihoods in the Middle Hills," *The Record* [October 9, 2017].

17 "Too Slow a Pace," *The Himalayan Times* [December 29, 2017].

18 Austin Lord, personal communication [January 20, 2017].

19 Galen Murton, *Border Corridors: Mobility, Containment, and Infrastructures of Development between Nepal and China* [University of Colorado, Department of Geography, 2017].

20 This work was fully funded by the US Fulbright Student Program. Though conceptual to date, efforts to develop a program for implementation in partnership with the shepherd community and local conservation organizations are ongoing.

21 Anthony Oliver-Smith, *The Martyred City: Death and Rebirth in the Andes* [Albuquerque: University of New Mexico Press, 1986], 15.

22 James Corner, *Recovering Landscape: Essays in Contemporary Landscape Theory* [Princeton: Princeton Architectural Press, 1999], ix.

shepherds as landscape-makers through the creation of an operationalized, hybrid knowledge database. Through daily ranging practice, they become intimately familiar with the contours and moods of the landscape. With a broadened scientific understanding of landscape dynamics built on this foundation of daily experience, they can guide the evolution of this landscape in response to emerging change. These proposals respond to vulnerability within the fabric of daily life by reducing the risk of livestock loss, easing demands placed on the landscape, expanding access to necessary resources, and making the case for an expansion of shepherd social capital.

The rangelands above Thini village all lie on south-facing mountainsides; forests on north-facing slopes make it difficult to keep track of flocks, and provide shelter from leopards. Sparse vegetation leaves the ground plane exposed to sun and wind, and forces shepherds and flocks to move continuously in search of fodder. Each portion of rangeland has a name and a *goth*, a set of seasonal shelters made from dry-stack stone. To provide more fodder, proposed infrastructures are designed to create moisture-preserving microclimates.[20] At Batang, a series of stone walls runs north-south to maximize shade, and curve toward the east at their downslope end to protect from the south-southwest wind. On the upslope tip of one wall, a small platform allows shepherds to gain a better vantage point while watching for predators, and the walls provide shelter for kids and lambs, which are hunted by eagles after birthing season.

The spring at another *goth*, Tanjomo, is one of few water sources in these rangelands. Shepherds often take entire flocks to the bottoms of deep river gorges to drink. A proposed spring house built underneath a boulder overhang encloses a small pool to provide shepherds with direct access to water for cooking. This pool overflows both into a watering trough outside the wall and a small swale to feed several *bhotepipal* [poplar] trees. In a landscape with a severe dearth of firewood, shepherds are forced to use juniper trees or the woody shrubs eaten by goats as fuel, and *bhotepipal* is a common local fuel source.

In the rangelands shared by Dzong, Chhyongkar, and Putak, the landscape is stressed by overgrazing. Increasingly sporadic and dramatic rainfalls, which rush down from surrounding mountains, have carved deep gashes in the ground, and storm surges are quickly lost in a landscape with very little water. Within one of these seasonal flowlines, a field of walls and small check dams is proposed. Check dams catch storm surges, charge groundwater, reduce erosion, and support fodder growth. Walls are placed on the windward side of each check dam to reduce evaporation by wind and sun. Though these walls interrupt visibility, existing wind shelters on surrounding hilltops provide ideal observation positions and sites for cooking a lunch of *dhindo* [buckwheat porridge].

A concrete canal runs past Chhyongkar to feed fields and a mill in Dzong. But outmigration has left many fields untended, and less water is now needed for irrigation. Both fuel and fodder are in dramatically short supply in the village, especially for landless shepherds unable to grow their own. They often resort to lighting shrubs on fire in the field to melt snow and stay warm during winter. Along this canal, a proposed series of tiered enclosures use surplus water to grow fuel and fodder. Stone from several nearby rockfalls and site-sourced soil provide building materials as at other sites. In each enclosure, the south-facing wall is made from adobe marked by deep triangular indentations. These accelerate the weathering process to gradually open the fodder-filled enclosures for musk deer and other species as grazing practice dwindles. As this shift occurs, driven by depopulation and climate change, shepherds must adapt or become unnecessary. Through continual adaptation and operationalization of this hybrid body of knowledge, they can situate themselves at the forefront of conservation practice by shaping the landscape in support of ecosystem function, species protection, and the reduction of human-animal conflict.

Describing post-avalanche change in a Peruvian highland village, Anthony Oliver-Smith argues that "we need our past. We are dependent upon it for understanding our present and for molding and adapting to our future, whatever uncertainties it may hold."[21] In a present defined by rapid change, these landscapes and the knowledge that drives them are foundations for the hybrid landscapes of the future. This hybridity will be found at the intersection of continuity and change through the mixing of knowledge, adaptive strategy, resources, and meaning. This landscape architecture practice "invoke[s] tradition and invention, the latter transforming and renewing the former."[22]

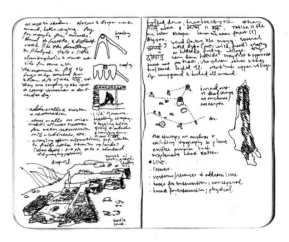

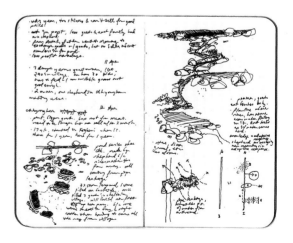

Pages from the author's notebooks.

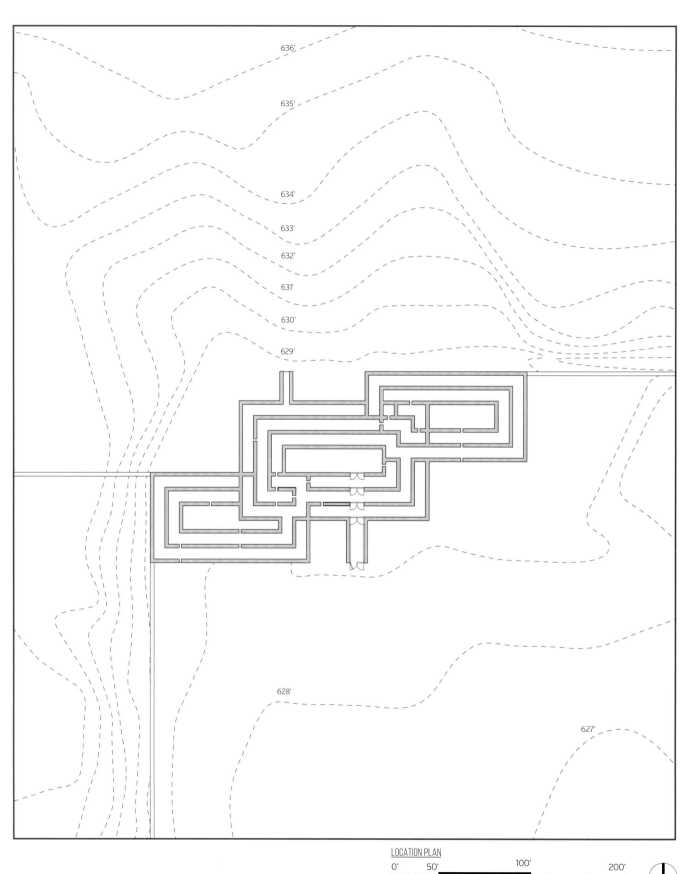

636'

635'

634'

633'

632'

631'

630'

629'

628'

627'

WALK THAT LINE
Thomas Oles

Thomas Oles is professor of landscape architecture and head of the Design Theory Group at the Swedish University of Agricultural Sciences, Uppsala, Sweden. He is the author of *Go With Me: 50 Steps to Landscape Thinking* (2013) and *Walls: Enclosure and Ethics in the Modern Landscape* (2014). His latest book, *Fieldwork in Landscape Architecture: Methods–Actions–Tools*, will be published by Routledge in 2019.

LANDSCAPE ARCHITECTURE, DESIGN

PROJECT NAME:

NO.	DATE.	REVISION:

SCALE: N/A   DRAWN BY: SK

DRAWING NUMBER

L1.0

Every profession is a club and a fortress. One way or another you will pay to get in. But once you are in, barring negligence or misconduct, you are in for life. The walls of this fortress do several important things. First, they exclude. Every profession is essentially a monopoly, protecting its members by inflating the value of their services in the marketplace. This means enforcing scarcity. Like the urban guilds of the Middle Ages, modern professions must regulate the number of aspirants allowed into them at any one time so that the supply of "professionals" always falls short of demand.

The gates of professions are guarded by the sentries of training and licensure. Even these fearsome twins would be toothless, however, without law. Here the fortress is unlike its medieval forebears. It is no island. Its influence extends far beyond its walls, and it has many allies. The most powerful of these is the state. States grant professions exclusive control over particular domains of formal knowledge; they allow the fortress to be built in the first place. But they also give them legal authority to prevent "amateurs" from selling the profession's goods *anywhere* in the economy. The reason for this is clear: those goods are widely seen as indispensable. Managing the technological and administrative complexity of modern industrial society is all but impossible without the formal knowledge and specialized skills that professionals possess. States and professions thus enter into a mutually beneficial transaction: legal status in exchange for public service. This transaction is assumed to be *disinterested*, removed at least in part from the exigencies of the market. Professionals may have to charge fees (they too must eat), but the god they serve is higher than mammon.

These aspects of professions have been acknowledged for over a century.[1] But there is something else about this fortress – something ultimately more important for understanding its power. Its walls are opaque. Like the monasteries from which their name originally derives, professions by definition are places hidden from general view. They may provide vital services to the *res publica*, but they themselves are anything but public in the word's original sense. On the contrary, every profession is, to one degree or another, a *secret* realm, a stronghold of mystical knowledge and arcane rites, radically separate from the mundane world. The walls marking this realm are no mere metaphor. At IBM in the 1960s, only a tiny, white-cloaked elect could go anywhere near the mainframes, receiving punch cards from lesser employees through a small window, then withdrawing to humming oracles whose messages only they might decode. This is a very particular case–the emergence of that scientific elite that Ralph E. Lapp called "the new priesthood"[2] –but it describes a characteristic of professions generally. No profession can be understood simply as a collection of people with similar knowledge and skills. Professions are, equally or even more, sacred domains in a profane world, their denizens the intermediaries through which modern people may still communicate with the divine when all the other gods are dead.

To place "design" in this stronghold (as in the phrase "design professions") is to make two assumptions. The first of these concerns the nature of design *itself*. Design, it says, is a distinct way of thinking and acting in the world, a mode of creating knowledge that spans or unites apparently dissimilar realms of human enterprise. Forget the obvious differences between designing a house, designing a smartphone interface, designing a watershed management plan, and designing a public transit system. What matters in each formulation is the gerund. The second assumption is that something about this particular way of thinking is inherently professional. Just as lawyers argue cases and surgeons perform operations (to take those most "professional" professions), designers *design things*. Whether these things are chairs, landscapes, or strings of code, the skills required to do so constitute a body of formal knowledge that is technically specific, hard to learn, and valuable to society. This entitles designers to the protections and rewards that professional enclosure affords.

The first assumption is plausible enough. There is ample reason to think that "design thinking" is fundamentally similar no matter what its object. But the second rings false. For one thing, if design is taken to mean the process of forming mental representations of possible worlds, one might reasonably view it as a universal–perhaps the essential–human impulse. As a recent book has argued, we are not *Homo sapiens* but rather *Homo prospectus*, born designers every one.[3] The phrase "design professions" might thus be seen as a category error, as vacuous in its own way as "language professions" or "tool-using professions." Professions are made up of people, and people speak languages and use tools, but this does not make language and tools themselves professional.

Even if one could establish that design is learned rather than innate, the notion that there exists some cohesive set of design professions would still be questionable. Indeed, it seems to contradict the first assumption above. What about non-design professions, like engineering or computer science, where design thinking is nevertheless routinely used? And what about all those design non-professions (here one thinks of the moat between landscape design and landscape architecture), surely far more numerous? If anything, design *qua* design is more closely allied with apprentice-based craft trades (what used to be called the mechanical arts) than with specialized domains like law or medicine. Even when its objects are abstract, design itself is always somehow worldly. Its original home is not the monastery but the guild.

And yet there is one way design does belong in that fortress. It is, at root, a mystery. For several decades now, a vast academic machinery has churned away attempting to analyze and quantify the design process. Add to this a veritable avalanche of popular copy devoted to the supposed powers of design thinking (when the *Harvard Business Review* gets in, you know there is money riding on the game).[4] And yet all this does not seem to have brought us much closer to understanding

GENERAL SYMBOLS

AREA OF DETAIL ENLARGEMENT

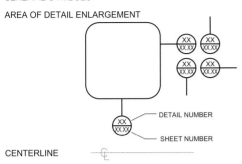

DETAIL NUMBER

SHEET NUMBER

CENTERLINE

DETAIL TAGS

DETAIL NUMBER

SHEET NUMBER

DRAWING TITLES

IDENTIFICATION
SCALE: XXXX = XX' - XX"

DIMENSION STYLE

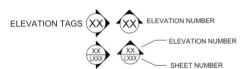

ELEVATION TAGS

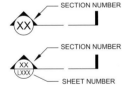

ELEVATION NUMBER

ELEVATION NUMBER

SHEET NUMBER

SECTION TAGS

SECTION NUMBER

SECTION NUMBER

SHEET NUMBER

ABBREVIATIONS

ADA	AMERICAN W/ DISABILITIES ACT
AL	ALIGN
ALT	ALTERNATE
ARCH	ARCHITECTURAL
@	AT
BLDG	BUILDING
BC	BOTTOM OF CURB
BO	BOTTOM
BOC	BEGINNING OF CURVE
BS	BOTTOM OF STAIR
BW	BOTTOM OF WALL
CAL	CALIPER
CEM.	CEMENT
CIP	CAST-IN-PLACE
CJ	CONTROL JOINT
C JT	CONSTRUCTION JOINT
CL	CENTERLINE
CLL	CONTRACT LIMIT LINE
COL	COLUMN
CONC.	CONCRETE
CONT.	CONTINUOUS
CUST.	CUSTOM
DIA	DIAMETER
DIM	DIMENSION
DG	DECOMPOSED GRANITE
DN	DOWN
DPR	DEPARTMENT OD PARKS & REC
DTL	DETAIL
DWG	DRAWING
E	EASTING
EA	EACH
EL	ELEVATION
ELEC	ELECTRIC
ENLGMT	ENLARGEMENT
EOC	END OF CURVE
EOS	EDGE OF SLAB
EQ	EQUAL
EQUIP	EQUIPMENT
EX, EXIST	EXISTING
EXP JT	EXPANSION JOINT
E-W	EAST WEST
FFE	FINISHED FLOOR ELEVATION
FIXT	FIXTURE
FL	FLOOR
FT	FOOT/FEET
FTG	FOOTING
FURN	FURNITURE
GA	GAUGE
GALV.	GALVANIZED
GEN	GENERAL
GL	GLASS
HORIZ	HORIZONTAL
HP	HIGH POINT
HR	HOUR
ID	INSIDE DIAMETER
IF	INSIDE FACE
JT	JOINT
L FIXT	LIGHTING FIXTURE
LOC	LOCATIONS
LP	LOW POINT
MAINT	MAINTENANCE
MAX	MAXIMUM
MECH	MECHANICAL
MEMB WP	MEMBRANE WATERPROOFING

LA+ DESIGN/SPRING 2019
87

WALK THAT LINE
Thomas Oles

PROJECT NAME:

NO.	DATE.	REVISION:

SCALE: N/A	DRAWN BY: SK

DRAWING NUMBER

L2.0

or communicating the actual *experience* of design. Despite efforts to rein it in, design remains substantially what Kevin Lynch and Gary Hack called it 40 years ago: "an irrational search, conducted over a ground prepared by experience."[5] This was no scholarly evasion; there is, quite simply, no recipe, no teachable method for becoming a "great" designer, only practice. On some fundamental level, design skill would seem to reside in a realm beyond the reach of human language – indeed, the greater the skill the less capable its possessor of explaining it.

These unsaid, nay *unsayable*, aspects of design, however real, were increasingly hard to defend amid the radical critique of "technocracy" and "task monopolies" that began in the 1960s.[6] This was particularly true for what started to be called, around the same time, "environmental design professions." Particularly in the case of architecture and planning, the authority of these professions was increasingly challenged by the publics whose interests they purported to serve. Much of this critique was directed at the depredations of what Jane Jacobs called the "pseudoscience of city planning."[7] Never again would it be possible for a professional to call the wholesale demolition of an urban neighborhood a "municipal hysterectomy" (as one banker did in reference to Boston's West End in 1960) and get away with it.[8] The priesthood was on notice, and it would be held to account.

In no other environmental design profession did this critique provoke as much soul searching as landscape architecture. The disciplinary response took two forms. The first was democratization, the opening up of once jealously guarded domains. In itself, this confers no particular distinction on landscape architecture. Professions are socially and politically constituted entities, and their walls are no defense against winds of change that happen to pass overhead. But landscape architecture was unusual in the zeal with which this agenda was pursued from inside the profession itself. Unlike urban planning or architecture, landscape architecture was not stormed by an angry mob; its gates were opened from the inside. True, landscape architects in practice may seldom have reached the upper rungs of the "ladder of participation,"[9] but their rhetoric, from the 1960s onward, soared in that direction.

Even as some were opening the gates of the fortress, others were busy shoring up the walls. For them, the problem with landscape architecture was not that it was too professional, but that it was not professional *enough*. The emerging field of ecology provided the basis for a new and very different set of disciplinary claims. Landscape architecture was to become the realm of what the historian Max Oehlschlaeger called "the imperial ecologists," a "science" to counter Jacobs's "pseudoscience."[10] No figure in this history looms larger than Ian McHarg, who saw the role of landscape architecture as averting ecological catastrophe. Like Garrett Hardin (whose "Tragedy of the Commons" article appeared within months of *Design with Nature* in 1969), McHarg was generally skeptical of citizens' capacity to do this themselves. But he was far more scathing when it came to "planetary diseases that have been institutionalized" in professions, "loathsome, almost beyond salvation."[11] Only a new technocracy could save the world from this old one. Landscape architecture must therefore become "overt, explicit, and replicable, just like a scientific experiment."[12]

These two visions of landscape architecture, easy to descry in the public pronouncements of the discipline (the 2016 "New Landscape Declaration" alludes in the space of a few paragraphs to both "understand[ing] the true complexity and holistic nature of the earth system" and "serv[ing] the health and well-being of all communities"), imply two distinct notions of design.[13] In one, design is a capacity shared by all people, a kind of common sense. In the other, it is a technical and scientific domain where methods are replicable and results are deduced in logical steps, "like an experiment." One might debate the respective virtues of these notions. One might aspire to their resolution, or argue that they are not really distinct at all. But whatever one's view of them, it is hard to see how either can avoid demystifying design itself. Both make design seem more rational, more prosaic, more secular than it really is.

The "New Landscape Declaration" states that landscape architecture is "charged with designing [the] common ground of landscape," but only the profession's most fervid advocates believe this. Landscape architecture must share authority and compete for influence with many other professions (and indeed many non-professions) responsible for shaping the human environment. From whence does our particular *authority* derive? If we embrace the notion of *Homo prospectus*, then our claim to legitimacy must be based on some additional set of skills and competences, some surplus above and beyond what citizens can do for themselves. What, exactly, are these? Are they technical skills? If so, which ones? Is it "holistic" thinking, and if so how can a rather vague habit of mind be monetized in the form of a professional service? Perhaps it is knowledge (as the "Declaration" puts it) of "environmental and cultural systems" or "complex social and ecological problems," a claim likely to be met with skepticism by sociologists and ecologists. Or is landscape architecture the one true meta-profession, a discipline of disciplines bringing "related professions together into new alliances" (the "Declaration" again) and liberating silo-bound specialists from their conceptual boxes?

It is an open question which of these answers, if any, is correct. Certainly some would seem less susceptible than others to the threat of automation. Given the pedestrian reality of most landscape architecture, with its relatively limited array of determining variables, can we really be certain that learning machines would do our job significantly worse? But even basing our professional authority on so-called soft skills, like facilitation among "different and often competing interest" (the Declaration again) is likely to leave us vulnerable. Do we

WALK THAT LINE
Thomas Oles

really want to have to argue that mediating among diverse and competing constituencies, leading "community design" processes, and the like, are tasks for which we are "uniquely positioned," a role for which we are better suited than any other? Perhaps, but then we must be ready, should our skills in this area be found wanting, to undertake the radical retooling of the profession–from education to licensing to practice–required to address the deficiency.

There is another way, a *simpler* way. If it hurts at all, it will only hurt for a minute. For ultimately none of the above claims, wherever they fall on the scale from technocracy to democracy, is a particularly solid ground on which to construct the professional edifice of landscape architecture. To say this is not to question their worthiness as aspirations or ethical principles. It is simply to say that, in using them to justify our existence, we sell ourselves altogether too cheaply. This is because, to a one, they relinquish the single most convincing argument we can make as "professionals": that *we know how to design landscapes. Homo sapiens* may indeed be *Homo prospectus*, but that does not mean everyone prospects equally well. We should not let commitment to justice or democracy (they are not the same) prevent us from saying, again and again, that we do this one thing better than others – both other people and other professions. What is more, we should never let our desire for legitimacy prevent us from affirming, loudly and unapologetically, the illogical, irrational, *mysterious* aspects of our work. Not everything about design can or must be articulated, not every design decision can or must be justified by "evidence." Far from a weakness, this represents our greatest professional strength in a logocentric and quantifying world. Design, unruly and mysterious, is one of a dwindling number of redoubts against the ever-marching armies of algorithms. We would do well to think long and hard about the risks to our authority, and perhaps our survival, before we pry open the profession's gates any further. For some gates, once opened, are not easily closed again.

People want their problems to be solved, but they also want to believe. Every professional, and certainly every design professional, must be a priest as well as a pragmatist. McHarg–eccentric, erratic, mystical, *visionary*–could walk that line. Can we?

1 Among the first to lay them out was Max Weber, in the so-called "Vocation Lectures" ("Politics as a Vocation" and "Science as a Vocation"), delivered in 1917 and 1918 respectively.

2 Ralph E. Lapp, *The New Priesthood: The Scientific Elite and the Uses of Power* (New York: Harper & Row, 1965).

3 Martin Seligman, et al., *Homo Prospectus* (New York: Oxford University Press, 2016).

4 Maya Bernstein, "*Plan a Better Meeting with Design Thinking*," Harvard Business Review (26 February 2018).

5 Kevin Lynch & Gary Hack, *Site Planning* (Cambridge MA: MIT Press, 1984), 139.

6 Albert W. Dzur, "Democratic Professionalism: Sharing Authority in Civic Life," *The Good Society* 13, no. 4 (2004): 6.

7 Jane Jacobs, *The Death and Life of Great American Cities* (New York: Random House, 1961), 13.

8 Medford Square TV, "The Lost Neighborhood" (1960), youtube.com/watch?v=c0eyYTajnA0 (accessed 30 April 2018).

9 Sherry R. Arnstein, "A Ladder of Citizen Participation," *Journal of the American Institute of Planners* 35, no. 4 (1969): 216–24.

10 Max Oelschlaeger, *The Idea of Wilderness: From Prehistory to the Age of Ecology* (New Haven: Yale University Press, 1991), 107.

11 Ian McHarg, *Man, Planetary Disease* (Washington: Agricultural Research Service, US Department of Agriculture, 1971), 4–5.

12 Ian McHarg, *A Quest for Life: An Autobiography* (New York: John Wiley & Sons, 1996), 341.

13 Landscape Architecture Foundation, "The New Landscape Declaration" (Washington: Landscape Architecture Foundation, 2016).

PROJECT NAME:

NO.	DATE.	REVISION:

SCALE: N/A DRAWN BY: SK

DRAWING NUMBER

L3.0

IN CONVERSATION WITH
JAMES CORNER

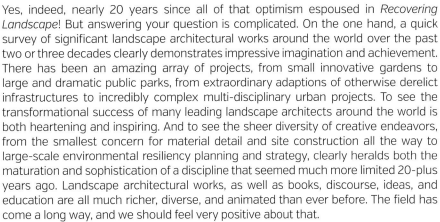

James Corner is an emeritus professor in landscape architecture and urbanism at the University of Pennsylvania School of Design, and founding partner of James Corner Field Operations. Since the early 1990s, Corner has assiduously combined the theory and practice of landscape architecture and is widely acknowledged as being a catalyst for the academic renaissance of the field in the early years of the 21st century. Through his teaching, writing, mapping, and now a significant body of built work, Corner has critically and yet optimistically advocated for the philosophical and practical relevance of the landscape architectural project to contemporary society. Conducting this interview for *LA+*, Richard Weller asked the questions he thought would be on readers' minds if they were to reflect on the arc of Corner's exceptional career.

+ By making a strong case for landscape as a medium, and for landscape architecture as a cultural project your 1999 edited volume *Recovering Landscape* effectively declared a renaissance for the field. We are now almost two decades into the 21st century, would you agree that things have significantly improved for landscape architecture?

Yes, indeed, nearly 20 years since all of that optimism espoused in *Recovering Landscape*! But answering your question is complicated. On the one hand, a quick survey of significant landscape architectural works around the world over the past two or three decades clearly demonstrates impressive imagination and achievement. There has been an amazing array of projects, from small innovative gardens to large and dramatic public parks, from extraordinary adaptions of otherwise derelict infrastructures to incredibly complex multi-disciplinary urban projects. To see the transformational success of many leading landscape architects around the world is both heartening and inspiring. And to see the sheer diversity of creative endeavors, from the smallest concern for material detail and site construction all the way to large-scale environmental resiliency planning and strategy, clearly heralds both the maturation and sophistication of a discipline that seemed much more limited 20-plus years ago. Landscape architectural works, as well as books, discourse, ideas, and education are all much richer, diverse, and animated than ever before. The field has come a long way, and we should feel very positive about that.

On the other hand, the same advancement could be said for many other fields, including those most closely related to landscape architecture: architecture and engineering. And at the same time, these fields have encroached upon landscape, poaching territory from landscape architects, who still, by comparison, seem to be behind the curve. Increased awareness about climate change, environmental challenges, and deteriorating ecological issues, combined with heightened anxieties about urbanization, public space, and social equity have created a new cross-disciplinary generation concerned with a focused agenda for design and creative work. Ian McHarg's *Design with Nature* (1969) seems especially prescient and relevant now, even though for decades it was held at arm's length by many landscape architects who preferred smaller-scale design and craft projects over the larger environment. Today, it seems as if everybody is focused upon solving the most challenging environmental and social issues of our time, with landscape architects still not quite at the forefront, even though their heritage and education suggests that they should be. Architects and engineers have taken on sustainability, resiliency, urbanism, and public space with an ambition and capacity that would have both impressed and shaken McHarg. Sure, there are still some excellent examples of landscape architects leading the way, and not all proposals put forward by architects and engineers are that credible or show deep understanding of the medium, but in the larger cultural sphere landscape architects do not figure as much as they ought. Their own discipline is being coopted, remade, and advanced by others.

For landscape architecture to regain its ground, landscape architects need to assume real leadership as opposed to subsidiary support; they need to become more critically aware, more aggressive, more entrepreneurial, and, frankly, more creative. *Recovering Landscape* remains an incomplete project.

+ Would you agree that compared to things like fashion, industrial design, and architecture for which constant innovation is the norm, landscape– particularly public landscape–seems to resist innovation in terms of form, materiality, and program? Could you speak to where innovation is located in the contemporary landscape project?

Yes, I would agree. The landscape medium is extraordinarily hard to continually reinvent. Unlike fashion, the duration of landscape is too long. Unlike industrial design, landscape has little commercial value; it is not a marketable product. Unlike architecture, the expression of landscape is horizontal and lacks immediacy, as well as clarity of understanding. Unlike the inorganic, hard, and synthetic materials of many design arts, the physical medium of landscape is unruly – a living, growing medium that takes on a life of its own, inevitably naturalizing and concealing any trace of human work or genius. Perhaps the most challenging issue is the fact that people do not see landscape as a design medium – they see landscape as countryside, nature, and passive background. People have a strong nostalgia or sentimentality for the pastoral landscape because it represents an antidote or salve to the perceived stresses of urbanization and work. Why innovate or change an already successful and desirable model, especially if this is seen as integral to heritage, locality, and place?

This conservatism is especially true given the increased emphasis today upon public consultation; as many open spaces and landscapes are public, it is only right that the public are actively consulted. However, the combination of "nimbyism," nostalgia, and fear of anything new or "out-of-place" results in predictable and benign design projects. Landscape is such a loaded and habitual medium that it inevitably retards its own advancement.

You ask where innovation might be located within the landscape project, and this is a good question. I believe that any innovation lies in the redefinition of landscape to begin with, for as long as landscape is still perceived as countryside, nature, and vegetation it has all the limitations described above. In this regard, Landscape Urbanism, for example, tries to conflate "landscape" with "city," to redefine both as one, a new hybrid. When urban layout, arrangement, infrastructure, program, and placemaking are viewed as "landscape"–as a complex system, both geometrical and dynamic–the possibilities for innovation are profound. Another form of redefinition occurs when you have a site or a condition that escapes any conventional notion of landscape. Something like the High Line, for example, does not lend itself immediately to a traditional notion of landscape – it is simultaneously infrastructure, architecture, and ruin. To see the High Line today as a landscape is not just its planting or greenery but more as a total conception, a holistically choreographed landscape armature, composed of steel, concrete, glass, plantings, birds, butterflies, people, places, events, programs, and atmospheres – all *designed*. The same could be said of various infrastructural, resiliency, ecological, and urban planning projects around the world, where landscape is no longer the planting bed, countryside, or natural setting, but something more holistic, cross-disciplinary, and transformative. These and other redefinitions of landscape set up the conditions for real innovation that is timely and relevant, suggesting new typologies, technologies, and programs.

Opposite: Fresh Kills Park, Staten Island, NY.

+ With their entries for the Parc de la Villette in 1984, Tschumi and Koolhaas abandoned landscape architecture's picturesque baggage. And yet, if one looks at the plans and perspectives being produced now by mainstream practices, one could be forgiven for thinking La Villette never happened. Can you reflect on this moment in the field's recent history and on its legacy?

Well, another good question, and one that actually expands upon what I was describing above. Landscape is so burdened by habit, sentimentality, and public expectation that it is extremely difficult to break the image. And yet the design proposals by Tschumi and Koolhaas for the Parc de la Villette were so extraordinary at the time because they did indeed redefine what a landscape could be. They did this not through formal or stylistic means but through an emphasis upon program. Landscape now was no longer scenery or setting but an operating system for alternative programming. The graphic representation, too, avoided the color green and any painterly effect. Tschumi's use of lilac, blue, red, and displaced cinematic perspective was both jarring and mesmerizing. Koolhaas's use of architectural line drawings supplemented by planimetric collages was both ruthlessly systematic and surrealistically eventful. Both projects deployed architectural precision with playful montage and performance, supplanting landscape as backdrop with landscape as program.

You raise the question of what happened next? Why no further development along these lines? Well, arguably, the Downsview Park competition (1999) produced a series of interesting alternative approaches, this time more ecologically informed. Similarly, Fresh Kills, Superkilen, and various other contemporary projects have provoked new possibilities while invoking new techniques and new ways of thinking. But, yes, you are right, the bulk of landscape architectural work still continues along traditional lines. The pastoral in particular is enjoying a huge renaissance today given the abundance of new large green and mostly passive parks around the world. And this is maybe okay – the pastoral has many great attributes: scenographic topography, meandering watercourses and softly edged lakes, large open lawns and meadows, clumps of majestic trees and plantings, lots of paths, journeys, and experiences throughout the seasons – a perfect respite from the bustling city. When done well (and they rarely are!), pastoral picturesque landscapes are timeless. But why so few alternatives?

I think the key reason it is hard for large urban landscapes to assume new and innovative dimensions is because public sentiment is more about traditional expectations than anything new. It is worth noting that la Villette was a professionally juried design competition: it did not engage public opinion or input. Indeed, since the building of the Parc de la Villette, many in the surrounding neighborhoods have yet to say much that is truly positive about it. They like the soccer fields and various other functions, but the image simply fails to resonate with the Parisian sense-of-place. And this may well be the clue to the very DNA of landscape – that landscape is always so deeply cued into place, time, and local culture. If you don't tap into that context, and you don't meaningfully include local people in the conception and execution of the project, it inevitably fails to resonate; it fails to feel grounded, of the place, and connected to the larger psycho-geographical context. I guess the trick would be in finding a way to deploy new kinds of redefinition of landscape not in isolation, but rather through rereading situational context, engaging in collective discussion, and leading a meaningful process through which something truly new and relevant might be created.

+ When you hold your design work up to your writing, what sort of connections or slippages do you see? Or, more broadly, what sort of gaps do you see between landscape architecture in theory and landscape architecture in practice, and do these gaps concern you?

This is a big question that probably deserves more time and attention than we have here in this short interview. One can certainly review my body of writing, which spans from representational interests to instrumentality and technique, and wonder whether or not the professional work of Field Operations lives up to the aspirations sought in the writing. But I don't think this is a fair measure. The writing, by definition, is theoretical and intended to expand thinking and understanding – it has no limits and

is autonomous, while the design work is inevitably practical, situated, and contingent. Theory informs practice, and practice informs theory, but there is rarely a mirror-like conflation of the two. A more accurate correspondence between theory and practice is not a direct cause-and-effect but more a set of values, a set of themes or topics that are explored in different media and contexts. In this regard, you could see issues of geography, place, technique, temporality, instrumentality, or craft playing out differently in both bodies of work, as well as a general search for what is essential to the landscape medium, both imaginary and physical, textual and material. Practices operate in and on the world, and in this case you could say that theory is always about the larger project, practice the specific performance.

+ In the academy, we like to think that representation can be revelatory and transformative, but in practice representation is largely measured by how well it communicates to a lay audience. You've been deeply engaged in both sides of this equation so could you speak to how you approach the problem of representation today?

Well, yes, you are right: representational technique is something that can help stimulate creativity during design conception while also communicating intent to others. In landscape architecture, both aspects of representation are critical. A sketch, a map, a digital model, a quick collage – all can help to direct thinking and shape ideas, all are critical for design development and ideation. At some point, these touch down to become the notational basis for project construction (measured plans, sections, axonometrics, technical 3-D models, etc), as well as the communication tool to convey intent to others (typically perspective renderings in concert with explanatory diagrams, models, and, increasingly today, animations).

A key challenge today is that the sheer speed and pervasive availability of digital media has led to a lot of copying and repetition – you can almost see precedents and references repeatedly played out in any project around the world; it is hard to find real originality. And a second challenge is the spell of the visual – the scenic rendition in all of its perfection deployed as a commercial selling tool. This has always been the case in both architecture and landscape architecture, but the sheer photorealistic completeness of the fully rendered image denies interpretation and possibility – it becomes the final (e)valuation of the project, a kind of superficial take at the expense of the many other technological, performative, programmatic, or other values hidden in the nonvisual aspects of the work. It also does not help to expand the public's appreciation for landscape as anything other than the picturesque – picturing inevitably promotes the desire for more of what is already recognizable and known.

Above: Paving detail collage of the Seattle Central Waterfront.

+ With its grand overviews from photographer Alex McLean, and your corresponding montages, your book *Taking Measures Across the American Landscape* (1996) held out the prospect of an expanded purview for landscape architecture – an engagement with large-scale working landscapes. A new generation of academics seems to have followed your lead in this regard, but for them (and by extension for the profession) getting a credible grip on this larger territory seems difficult. Do you think the profession should now just accept a certain territorial limitation, or should we continue the struggle for more?

Taking Measures Across the American Landscape was an amazing eye-opening experience. I learnt how radically different the American landscape is from the more layered, historical, and culturally ingrained landscapes of Europe and Britain. On the one hand is the issue of scale, space, and geometry, but more fundamental is the issue of pure instrumentality. The American Landscape is brutally pragmatic, the consequence of building utility and economy before any kind of cultural heritage. This work stimulated a whole set of design studios at Penn in the 1990s focused upon infrastructural landscapes, regional landscapes, and large ecosystems. And, as you mention, others too have since explored the potential of thinking bigger and expanding landscape architectural scope.

The challenge to larger scale work is simply that one needs a more centralized and long-term form of governance. The big social and environmental issues of our time cannot be resolved at a local level alone: they require much larger scale efforts and cross-jurisdictional coordination. Land and infrastructure planning is a state dependent activity, with an activist government capable of enacting clear decisions, regulations and controls. In a democracy, and especially in a republic such as the United States, it is practically impossible for coherent, long-term, and effective land planning to be done with any consistent clarity.

+ Peter Walker was recently quoted in *The Dirt* as saying "I will not talk about a region or ecology – we've had enough of that." One infers from this dismissal of both scale and environmental crises that, for him at least, ecology, design, and planning are still fundamentally incompatible. In contrast, you and others resolved this old tension between regional planning and design-as-art by rereading ecology as akin to creativity. After 20 years of practice do you think Walker has a point, or are we yet to see an ecological aesthetic?

I would like to see the context of that quote – I don't believe that Walker is as averse to either planning or ecology as the quote in isolation might suggest. On the other hand, he is absolutely committed only to mid- and small-scale projects, largely because these are the majority of real projects out there, and also because they have their own set of complications that require real expertise and skill at that scale of design and implementation. He might be suggesting that large-scale environmental concerns are beyond the landscape architect's scope, given the importance of policy, regulation, and economics rather than design per se, and therefore just a distraction to the everyday concerns of most landscape architectural practices.

Regardless, the question remains, can there be a more-productive dialogue between regional planning and site design, and between ecological interests and artistic expression? I have to assert that of course there can, and I believe that the best leading practices today are mediating these various scales and interests. I am thinking of Kongjian Yu's work in China, for example, and this scale of work may only be possible given the state authority of China, but nonetheless it does describe real world projects that are conflating planning, design, and ecology as one synthesis.

+ You were a formative part of the development of the discourse that became known as Landscape Urbanism. Now that the "movement" has somewhat dissipated, what do you think it achieved or may yet achieve?

Landscape Urbanism suffered from too much academic advancement, too quickly and too divergently. Read most of the texts and manifestos today and they point in myriad directions, excited and optimistic, yet unfocussed and imprecise. And yet I still deeply believe that hybridizing landscape with urbanism allows for a more significant role for landscape architects in the shaping of the future city. While traditional planners and architects tend to view the city as a set of objects, more-or-less fixed, landscape architects bring a richer complex systems dynamic to bear on how we represent, think about, and shape the city. After all, the city functions like a natural ecosystem – it shrinks and expands in time, with many various systems of mobility, supply, waste, and program all interacting together. Like natural systems, the city comprises a dynamic amalgam of patches, corridors, matrices, and geometrical frameworks that support various forces and flows of matter and energy. Taught in ecological systems, together with various techniques of mapping and organizing, many landscape architects are capable of seeing and shaping the city as a dynamic organism as distinct from a fixed object. Field replaces figure and object.

Similarly, urbanism reconditions landscape. Landscape is now not just green open space but more fundamentally the whole operating system upon which a city functions. Landscape is still the space in-between, and still the domain of parks and public spaces, but it is also the source of food and energy, water and waste management, mobility infrastructure, resiliency structures, and frameworks for development. It is worth continuing to advance Landscape Urbanism as something more comprehensive and effective than traditional planning and architectural models of the past.

+ In their somewhat mistaken critique of landscape urbanism, Andrés Duany and Emily Talen took aim at the High Line as a boutique project that venerated the modernist curse of the overhead walkway. They argued instead that money should have been spent on fixing the streets below. Others accuse the High Line of perpetuating gentrification, and some worry over it as a model of heavily regulated public space. How do you respond to these criticisms?

I find most of the doctrine of New Urbanism boring and dogmatic. I appreciate the original moment in the 1980s when New Urbanism was taking hold—as a kind of alternative to the brutal megastructures of modernist urban planning, providing a guiding vision for human-scaled walkable neighborhoods, clear hierarchies of space, territory (public–private), and open space frameworks – but it has since devolved into too restrictive a set of rules and controls that limits variation and innovation.

The critique of the High Line as taking people off the streets below, and taking money away from the improvement of the streets, is not only a cheap shot but wholly irrelevant in the context of urban Manhattan. The point might be well taken in the context of a small town where you would never have sufficient numbers of people to warrant both overhead and street-level walks, but both the High Line and its street level neighborhood see millions of people every year.

The gentrification criticism of the High Line is also a little glib and fast. Sure, the High Line has played a part in the development of surrounding blocks and buildings with new expensive housing and spaces, but so too did many other measures, including a massive rezoning and economic incentive program that encouraged new building development. Neighborhood displacement has been at least partially alleviated by affordable-housing requirements, as well as various public grants and support systems. Some would argue that the significant economic return to the city through all of this new development has subsequently allowed the city to spend revenue on schools, low income housing, and other investments throughout the various boroughs. It is all far from perfect, but it is not fair to blame or denigrate the High Line for all of this economic transition. In fact, the High Line remains the most open, accessible, and inclusive public space threading across the west side of Manhattan. People strolling along there are from all walks of life, all economic and ethnic groups, all ages and abilities, and all interests and biases. This cosmopolitan spectacle is what makes the High Line so fascinating, as diverse peoples are all exposed cheek-by-jowl with one another, promenading together, enjoying the sights and sounds of the city, while both exhibiting and viewing one another. It is neither an exclusive space, nor glitzy and elite; it is instead open to all, welcoming, and engaging. Moreover, the significant efforts by the Friends of the High Line to provide cultural and community programming further promotes diversity, inclusion, and mutual participation. The facts simply do not support those who want to say the High Line is all about gentrification; to the contrary, it has fostered and created a whole new space of exposure, encounter, fun, and delight for all.

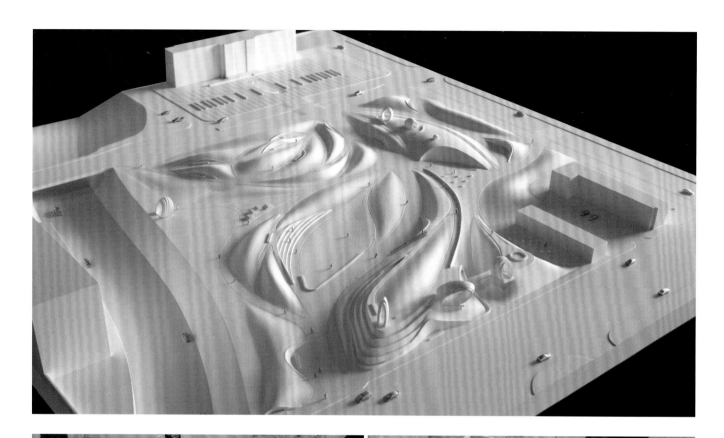

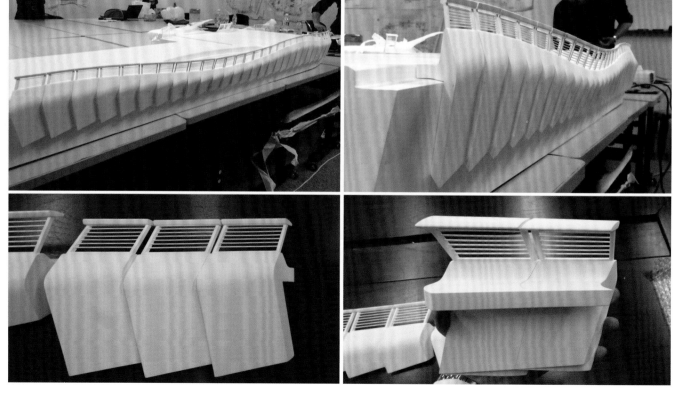

+ You've spent almost equal time in the academy and practice and have been witness to the best in both. What can they do better?

The academy is a place to grow and advance the imagination. It is a place without boundaries, a place full of possibilities. Helping a student learn the rudiments of our discipline, while at the same time expanding their critical thinking skills, their capacity for creativity and invention, their aptitude for leadership, and their understanding and appreciation of the medium, occurs best in the open environment of the academy. Here, constraints are removed precisely in order to allow possibility to be explored and articulated. The academy is by definition theoretical because it is a place to nurture ideas, stimulate creativity, and provoke growth.

Practice, on the other hand, is immersion in the real world. Each project has a host of highly situated, specific contingencies. As mentioned earlier, theory does not work here so perfectly because of the messiness of any given real-world situation. A judge of law must in practice be situational, evaluating each case on its own unique set of facts, while in law school they were most likely engaged with highly theoretical propositions and hypotheticals. The same is true in our work with projects, where we have clients, stakeholders, communities, politics, budgets, social relationships, site conditions, schedules, events, and transactions. A day's work in practice is inevitably about negotiating myriad complications. As with the judge, theoretical work in school is fundamental to developing the kind of critical thinking skills and mental agility to deal with the complexity of day-to-day reality in practice.

What both the academy and professional practice could do better is to recognize the fundamental necessity for meaningful dialogue between these two worlds. The academy need not be so exclusive and critical, diminishing practice as "commercial" or "conventional." In turn, practice need not be so cynical and restrictive, diminishing the academy as "irrelevant" and "intellectual." Both need to work together to find a real synergy and dialogue, recognizing that both worlds are essentially practices: they both seek to operate in and on the world, less as commentary and more as action.

+ In the last issue of LA+ we asked landscape historians what they thought would be the main themes when the history of the 21st century of landscape architecture is written. What do you think?

Urbanism – for the city is the only viable solution to growing populations, diminishing resources, and equitable economies.

Ecology – for this is the only means to properly understand and operate with the myriad complex dynamic forces that characterize both social and natural systems, avoiding silos and walls while creating open platforms.

Garden – for at root, the philosophy and poetics of the garden (time, place, tactility, nature, reflection, cultivation, earth, pleasure, surprise) are the most fundamental aspects of landscape architecture and its contribution to society.

Opposite, above: Physical model of Tongva Park in Santa Monica, CA.

Opposite, below: Study models for the Hong Kong Victoria Dockside.

A Report to an Academy

Jennifer Zell is a Senior Associate at AHBE Landscape Architects in Los Angeles. She has worked on a wide range of project types and scales including ecological restoration, urban design, and recreation planning. This piece is a take on Franz Kafka's short story "A Report to an Academy," where an ape reflects on his experience of becoming a human and of the subversion of his ape nature necessary to survive and thrive in the world of men. Here, Zell rewrites Kafka's story from the viewpoint of a female in the field of landscape architecture.

Honored Members of the Academy!

You have done me the honor of inviting me to give your Academy an account of the life I formerly led as a female.

It has been 25 years since I first entered my professional training and came to understand the necessity of casting off my former female self to become male. This transformation was achieved with the help and encouragement of excellent instructors, mentors, and friends. I could never have achieved what I have accomplished had I stubbornly stuck to my youthful notions of being. The early years of my professional life is when the battle to transform raged the hardest. It was difficult to cut away the feminine flesh from my bones when it was pulsing with biological prowess and it took tremendous self-discipline to subvert its force. Decades later the fragments of my former female self are nearly erased as the biological rhythms and dark seductive powers have diminished with age and neglect.

The first thing I learned was to wear pants. At first uncomfortable, bunching and pulling in the wrong places, today, standing at the peak of my career, they are like a second skin. I can't overstate how important wearing pants was in entering and establishing myself in the world of men. For the story of my training I will begin at the place of my first employment. After being hired, I worked long hours at below poverty level pay to prove my gratitude for the opportunity to work for The Great Male Founder. One of the men hired at the same time had the habit of making requests of me to make copies or fetch coffee for him; he was a dedicated instructor and patiently showed me how he was accustomed to having females complete these tasks for him. As I look back now, it seems during this time a cage was erected around me from which escape was not possible. One wall of the cage was erected upon discovering that the route to success for a female was to seduce powerful men. For evidence of this truth, I have only to recall how it was universally understood that the female principal had gained her position by sleeping with The Great Male Founder. To believe the logic that talent and hard work merited such advance was naïve and absurd.

Over time, I learned to closely mirror the behavior of the men around me and I acquired a calmness which kept me from trying to escape, but soon I received a forceful blow from one of my trainers – a move I had not anticipated. I was given a pink slip, along with three female coworkers, for what was later understood as our condition of being female and youthful enough to complicate working. The four of us had not seduced The Great Male Founder: that individual remained in her position as long as the affair continued, as did all the male employees. The men were good creatures and in spite of it all, I harbor no lingering ill will toward them. When I encounter these former male coworkers—as I occasionally do so many years later, congratulating them as they receive the professional awards of excellence and fellowship that is their natural destiny—my feelings are not all hateful.

My most remarkable achievement was growing a beard. Uncomfortable and repulsive to me at first, I have grown fond of this symbol of masculinity and freedom and the effect it produces at construction sites. It is scratchy, hot, and demands daily grooming and attention, but with it I have gained the respect and good humor of the men who now take great satisfaction in my transformation.

Admittedly, my transformation was not without setbacks. At the moment when the walls of my cage compressed the tightest, I was unable to fight my nature and produced and cared for two children. That youthful lapse into female being has cost me, I am told, a 37% reduction in my earning power.[1] Even with this setback, I have crossed the evolutionary divide in 25 short years. There was no attraction for me in imitating the men I observed; rather like Kafka's ape, I needed a way out, "even should the way out prove to be an illusion."[2]

Reflecting on what I have accomplished, with my hands in my pants pockets and my beard handsomely manicured, I find it exhilarating that I have managed to reach the level of an average man. After my routine daily performance, and after I have drunk my whiskey and eaten my dinner, I admit, I cannot bear to look in the mirror. In my reflection, I see a softness returning to the corners of my eyes, which by next morning must be forced back to the invisible places of my body. On the whole, at any rate, I have achieved what I set out to achieve. Was it worth the trouble? This is not a question I will answer for the honored Members of the Academy; I am only making a report.

1 Sylvia Hewlett & Carolyn Luce, "Off-Ramps and On-Ramps: Keeping Talented Women on the Road to Success," *Harvard Business Review* (March 2005).
2 Franz Kafka, *The Metamorphosis and Other Stories* (New York: Schocken Books Inc., 1948), 178.

RICHARD WELLER
TERRARIUM
THE ULTIMATE DESIGN EXPERIMENT

Richard Weller is Professor and Chair of Landscape Architecture at the University of Pennsylvania where he also holds the Martin and Margy Meyerson Chair of Urbanism. Weller is author of a number of books on design and regional planning including *Boomtown 2050: Scenarios for a Rapidly Growing City* (2009) and *Made in Australia: The Future of Australian Cities* (2014). His recently published *Atlas for the End of the World* (2017) documents global flashpoints between urbanization and biodiversity.

+ TECHNOLOGY, DESIGN

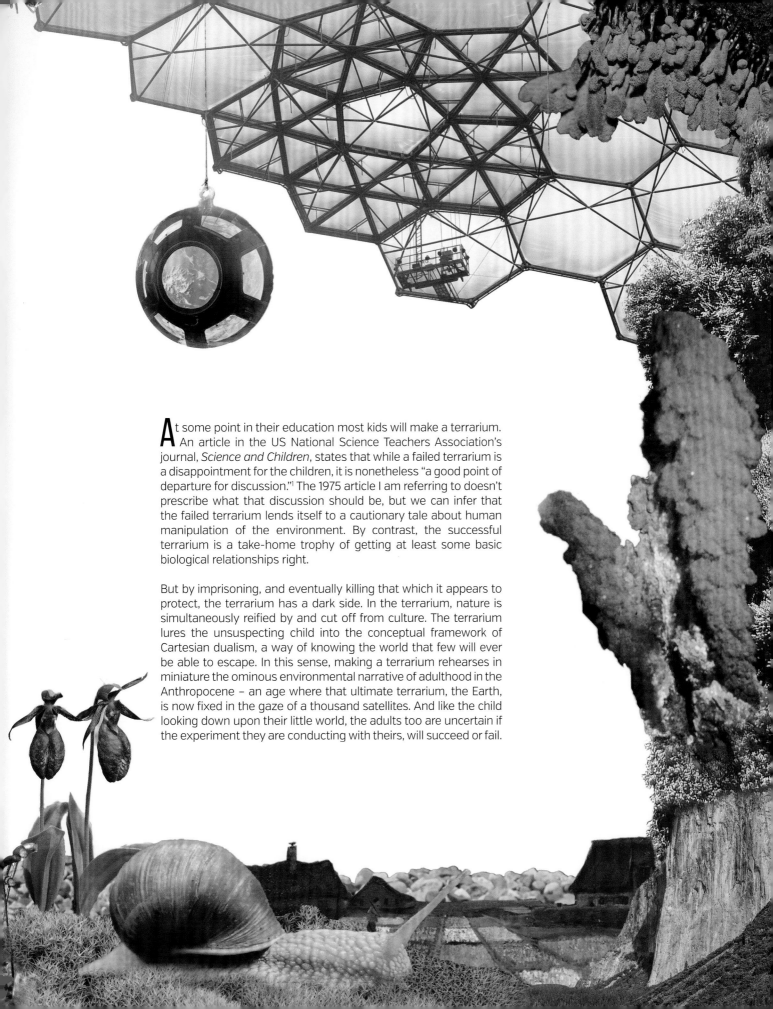

At some point in their education most kids will make a terrarium. An article in the US National Science Teachers Association's journal, *Science and Children*, states that while a failed terrarium is a disappointment for the children, it is nonetheless "a good point of departure for discussion."[1] The 1975 article I am referring to doesn't prescribe what that discussion should be, but we can infer that the failed terrarium lends itself to a cautionary tale about human manipulation of the environment. By contrast, the successful terrarium is a take-home trophy of getting at least some basic biological relationships right.

But by imprisoning, and eventually killing that which it appears to protect, the terrarium has a dark side. In the terrarium, nature is simultaneously reified by and cut off from culture. The terrarium lures the unsuspecting child into the conceptual framework of Cartesian dualism, a way of knowing the world that few will ever be able to escape. In this sense, making a terrarium rehearses in miniature the ominous environmental narrative of adulthood in the Anthropocene – an age where that ultimate terrarium, the Earth, is now fixed in the gaze of a thousand satellites. And like the child looking down upon their little world, the adults too are uncertain if the experiment they are conducting with theirs, will succeed or fail.

Seen through the contemporary filter of an atmosphere now overloaded with greenhouse gases, it is fitting that terrariums have their origin in and were inspired by a desire to protect delicate plants, not only from winter, but also from the heavily polluted atmosphere of Victorian London. There, the surgeon and amateur horticulturalist Nathaniel Bagshaw Ward accidentally "discovered" what would become known as Wardian cases: enclosed glass containers that permitted plants to thrive without external inputs.[2] Wardian cases became popular when in 1834 J.C. Louden, the editor of *The Gardeners' Magazine*, enthusiastically presented them to his readership. Through miniaturization, the Wardian case made accessible and domestic what had hitherto been the aristocratic and scientific domain of large glasshouses. Ward also speculated that his cases could have therapeutic benefit, as well as the capacity for food production to improve the diet of the urban poor, both of which have now been proven to some extent true.

However, as is the case with all human modifications of the environment, benefits are shadowed by problems. For example, the Wardian case enabled the globalization of agriculture by distribution of specimens throughout the British Empire, but also unwittingly facilitated the transplantation of species that would later be cursed as "invasives." Additionally, from a postcolonial perspective, Louden's premonition of the efficacy of Ward's invention reads as insidious when he extrapolates that "perhaps the time may arrive when such artificial climates will not only be stocked with appropriate birds, fishes, and harmless animals, but with examples of the human species from the different countries imitated...who may serve as gardeners or curators of the different productions. But this subject is too new and strange to admit of discussion, without incurring the ridicule of general readers."[3] With the World's Exhibition of 1851 set inside Joseph Paxton's Crystal Palace–itself a mammoth terrarium– Louden's vision of the world's ecoregions and cultures as a theme park moved closer to reality. Notably, among the exotica of empire on display was one of Ward's own curiosities – a bottle sealed and unopened for 18 years containing a specimen of living moss.

Far more than a Victorian curiosity, the architectural typology of the terrarium and its latent fantasies of total environmental control refracts through the 20th century in iconic projects such as Buckminster Fuller's Dome over Manhattan (1960) and his US Pavilion in Montréal (1967), Walt Disney's Experimental Prototypical Community of Tomorrow (EPCOT) (1982) in Orlando, and, most infamously, Biosphere II in Arizona (1991). In this article, we will briefly revisit these precedents, but to truly understand the portent of the terrarium we will also follow its manifest destiny beyond the bubble of our own atmosphere, out into space.

Experiments on Earth

The most famous 20th-century architect of the terrarium was, of course, Buckminster Fuller. Fuller conceptualized and, through his Dymaxion cartography, unpacked the whole planet as a kind of geodesic dome and put it back together again as an architectural kit. Fuller advocated the use of geodesic domes from the scale of (affordable) housing to that of whole cities. While unsuccessful as mass housing, and often derided in terms of architectural aesthetics, the domes were and still are utilized by the military and other agencies as cost-effective, lightweight structures. More than this, the geodesic dome came to signify Fuller's particular brand of techno-utopian optimism, adopted by the ecological sub-culture of the 1960s and 1970s.

THE VIVARIUM; OR, INSECT-HOME.

FOR OBSERVING THE TRANSFORMATIONS OF BUTTERFLIES, MOTHS, AND OTHER INSECTS.

Fuller's lifelong engagement with the typology of the terrarium is best expressed by two iconic projects: the unbuilt Dome over Manhattan (1960) and the US Pavilion built for the 1967 Expo in Montréal. The two-mile-wide Dome over Manhattan, conceived in association with the architect Shoji Sadao, was intended to be a climate controlled and energy efficient bubble floating above the ground plane. How Fuller took this idea seriously is something of a mystery, as the incongruity of the dome with the surrounding grid raises awkward and unresolved questions of the relationship between the two. Covering a conventional exhibition building, the geodesic dome of the US Pavilion at the 1967 Expo in Montréal is a miniature version of the Manhattan concept. Here the architectural double entendre of placing a building inside a building performs the same "world within a world" trick as the terrarium; but instead of encasing nature, Fuller's utopia (the dome) and America's cornucopia (the exhibition) are brought into alignment. After the Expo, the dome briefly housed botanical displays before a fire in 1976 melted its plastic skin, spewing plumes of thick black smoke into the sky. Renamed and redeemed as "the Biosphere," it now houses exhibitions about the environment and climate change.

By this time, Fuller's technological cathedrals had caught the eye of that eternal American optimist, Walt Disney. Six years after Fuller and Sadao had sketched their Dome over Manhattan, Disney set about making the vision a reality, only now on a 50-acre tabula rasa in Orlando, Florida. Titled the "Experimental Prototype Community of Tomorrow" (EPCOT), the dome was intended to house a community free of urban blight, congestion, and pollution. According to the propaganda, EPCOT would be "protected day and night from rain, heat and cold, and humidity" and offer "employment for all."[4] As Andrew Hurbner describes it, through the "benevolent control of downtown spaces, homes, transportation, and greenways" EPCOT would "stave off slum formation, poverty, and blight, and with them, urban riots like those that had rocked Los Angeles in 1965 and several other major cities in 1966."[5]

Soon after pitching the project, however, Disney died, leaving EPCOT to become the tragicomedy one might expect when entrusting utopia to theme park executives. When it opened in 1982, EPCOT's most prominent feature was a vast carpark, and the all-encompassing dome had contracted into what looked like a giant golf ball. Named "Spaceship Earth" in deference to Fuller's eponymous book, the dome now houses an audio-animatronic ride designed by the science fiction writer Ray Bradbury.[6] As Bradbury explained to journalists in 1977, guests are taken on a 15-minute tour of the entirety of universal history, shown how to "clean the air, unpollute [sic] the seas and save the whales." At the end of the tour guests are asked "what is our future?" Bradbury's answer: "we have to go into space."[7]

Spurred on by the Cold War, serious preparation for this apparent inevitability gained momentum internationally around the same time that Fuller's geodesic domes, and his metaphor of "Spaceship Earth" entered popular culture. In fits and starts both the Russian and American space programs developed closed-system simulation programs involving plants, animals, and humans.[8] The first, in 1965, was the Russian Bios-1 experiment where the atmosphere necessary to sustain one person in a 12 m3 enclosure was generated by an algal cultivator containing *Chlorerra vulgarus*. Bios-1 achieved 20% self-sufficiency. To improve upon this, in 1968 Bios-2 expanded the experiment's territory to include an additional 8.3 m3 area containing a diversity of edible plants. Then, built entirely underground, at a capacious 315 m3, Bios-3 attempted to simulate off-planet conditions for up to three people; the best it could achieve was to sustain two people for a maximum of five months.[9] Because additional nutrition in the form of animal products and electric energy to power xenon lamps for plant growth were supplied from outside, these experiments failed to achieve self-sufficiency in conditions of absolute isolation. What these closed-system experiments underscore is how complex and difficult it is to create bioregenerative systems, and by extension just how much of our daily biochemical existence in the open system of the Earth we take for granted. NASA, too, had been experimenting with similar prototypes to the Russians during the 1960s and '70s but it was the privately funded and designed Biosphere II in Oracle, Arizona that turned the science of bioregenerative life support systems into a public spectacle. Replete with simulations of the world's major biomes and spanning 1,900 m2, Biosphere II (Biosphere I being the actual Earth) was the McMansion of closed systems or, as Roy Walford put it, "the Garden of Eden on top of an aircraft carrier."[10] On September 26, 1991, eight "biospherians" or "terranauts" as they were variously called, including Walford, entered the enclosure and didn't come out until two years later. By the time they emerged, the ecosystem had virtually collapsed, all pollenating insects had died, cockroaches had overtaken, oxygen levels were diminished, and the crew had broken into warring factions. However, there were some positive findings: individuals recorded some health improvements, 83% food self-sufficiency was achieved, and much was learned about our capacity (or rather, incapacity) to design and manage ecosystems.[11]

Experiments in Space

As a container isolating and protecting plant life, the terrarium has a crucial role to play both metabolically and psychologically for humans undertaking long duration flights and living for extended periods in space stations and off-planet settlements. However, as the scientific literature attests, growing a humble lettuce in space is no simple thing: it means light, water, oxygen, carbon dioxide, temperature, and nutrition need to be precisely, and constantly, controlled.

The first terrarium containing a variety of plants in space was the "Oasis" greenhouse on Salyut 1, the first space station launched in 1971 by the USSR. Since then, terraria of one sort or another have been included in all space stations to study the potential of plants in micro-gravity conditions to supplement space traveler diets, filter air, cleanse waste water, and provide medicinal treatments. In 1975, Salyut 4 took the honor of hosting the first vegetable garden in space, and in 1982 aboard Salyut 7 the first flower in space was cultivated.[12] The Salyut missions also produced the first space-farmers of note, in particular Valentin Lebedev who, during his 211 days onboard Salyut 7, cultivated peas, lettuces, tomatoes, coriander, and onions. The first work of what we might call landscape architecture in space—that is, a garden designed "for the sole purpose of ornamental plant culture to provide psychological comfort to the cosmonauts"—was a terrarium built into the structure of Salyut 6 as a small picture window.[13] The current International Space Station has a fully automated micro-gravity garden the size of a suitcase, which contains more than 180 sensors relaying real-time information back to NASA's Kennedy Space Center.[14]

What all this research points toward is the prospect of building controlled, ecological life-support systems, replete with fertile soil, insects, animals, and plants, which could sustain large numbers of people indefinitely; in short, the colonization of other planets. Taking Mars as an example, however, the challenges are significant. On Mars, gravity is 1/100th of what it is on Earth, there is no readily available water, no nitrogen, the regolith contains aluminum (which is toxic to plants), and, in comparison to Earth, the climate is extreme. Furthermore, since it currently costs about $10,000 to put a pound of payload into Earth's orbit, launching even a modest pot-plant into space is prohibitively expensive.[15] But instead of hauling organic materials into space, NASA is asking if we could just grow them there. Just as life was once seeded on Earth, if the initial conditions could be sparked on other planets, then life's self-generative capacity could be harnessed.

Lynn Rothschild from the Ames Research Center is confident that biological engineering can overcome the challenges of creating life-support systems for humans in space.[16] It all begins with what she refers to as a "PowerCell." These designer cells would use solar radiation to convert carbon dioxide, nitrogen, water, and minerals into organic compounds such as sugars and proteins. Thus, she claims, "by the end of the decade, we will have taken the first steps towards realizing the vision of a synthetic biology enabled future off planet...Using organisms as feedstock, additive manufacturing through bioprinting will make possible the dream of producing bespoke tools, food, smart fabrics, and even replacement organs on demand."[17]

Beginning with the Wardian cases that enabled the British Empire to relocate tea production from China to India, to the creation of entirely new ecosystems in space, the seemingly innocent terrarium contains some of our wildest dreams and delusions. Today's equivalent to the classroom terrarium experiment with which this article began is a commercially available product known as the "Space Garden." The Space Garden is described by its manufacturers as "a ground-based version of the vegetable growth system designed for the International Space Station."[18] As advertised, the "Space Garden comes with all the materials needed to conduct biological agricultural and life science investigations, just like the astronauts. Each kit includes an expandable growth chamber, seeds, watering syringe, growth medium, and educational activities to introduce the science of plants in space in a fun – even an edible way!" And as it was in 1975 with school kids innocently fumbling over their terraria, when a Space Garden fails in today's classroom we can assume it will also trigger useful discussion. Only now, the teacher might have to explain that the terrarium experiment is not just a little symbol of the world, it is the world.

Acknowledgment
The author thanks Christopher Feinman
for research assistance on this paper.

1 V. Daniel Ochs & Mary R. Brock "Bottle Biology," *Science and Children* 13, no. 2 (1975): 15–17.

2 David R. Hershey, "Doctor Ward's Accidental Terrarium," *The American Biology Teacher* 58, no. 5 (1996): 276-81. As for Ward's "discovery" there is evidence to suggest that the ancient Greeks and Romans had enclosed plants with rudimentary forms of glass to force growth.

3 John Claudius Loudon, *Remarks on the Construction of Hot-Houses* (London, 1817), 4 quoted in William Taylor, "The Cultivation of Reason: Functionalism and the Management of Nature" *Studies in the History of Gardens & Designed Landscapes* 18, no. 2 (1998): 130.

4 Andrew J. Huebner, "The Conditional Optimist: Walt Disney's Postwar Futurism," *The Sixties* 2, no.2 (2009): 227–44.

5 Ibid.

6 Buckminster Fuller, *Operating Manual for Spaceship Earth* (New York: Pocket Books, 1968).

7 John C. Tibbetts, "Ray Bradbury's EPCOT Adventure," *Storytelling* (2006): 57, at 60.

8 Frank B. Salisbury, Josef I. Gitelson & Genry M. Lisovsky, "Bios-3: Siberian Experiments in Bioregenerative Life Support," *BioScience* 47, no. 9 (1997): 575–85.

9 Ibid., 578.

10 Jordan Fisher Smith, "Life Under the Bubble," *Discovery Magazine* (October 2010) http://discovermagazine. com/2010/oct/20-life-under-the-bubble (accessed July 22, 2018).

11 Now owned and managed by the University of Arizona, Biosphere II is part tourist attraction, part white elephant, and part Landscape Evolution Observatory (LEO). In what appears to be an experiment relevant to terraforming alien environments or repairing those we have denuded here on earth the LEO consists of three artificial landscapes made up of as little preexisting organic material as possible. These are rigged with 1800 sensors monitoring how biomass changes over time: Luke A. Pangle, et al., "The Landscape Evolution Observatory: A Large-Scale Controllable Infrastructure to Study Coupled Earth-Surface Processes," *Geomorphology* 244 (2015) 190–203.

12 Sandra Haeuplik-Meusburger, et al., "Greenhouses and their Humanizing Synergies," *Acta Astronautica* 96 (2014): 148–50.

13 Robert Zimmerman, "Growing Pains: It's the One Area of Space Science in Which You Get to Eat the Experiment, *Air & Space Magazine* (September 1, 2003).

14 NASA, "Orbiting Agriculture," https://www.nasa.gov/ missions/science/f_lada.html (accessed July 22, 2018).

15 Lynn J. Rothschild, "Synthetic Biology Meets Bioprinting: Enabling Technologies for Humans on Mars (and Earth)" *Biochemical Society Transactions* 44, no. 4 (2016): 1158–64.

16 Ibid.

17 Ibid.

18 Space Garden, http://www.spacegarden.net (accessed July 22, 2018).

Top: BIOS-3, Krasnoyarsk, 1972.

Middle: Biosphere II, 2008.

Bottom: Space Garden, Orbital Technologies Corporation.

Previous page: Montréal Biosphère, May 1976.

A is for Anthropocene

Paul A. Rodgers + Craig Bremner

A is for Anthropocene

An A–Z of Design Ecology

Craig Bremner is Professor of Design at Charles Sturt University, Australia. He holds a Master of Design and a PhD in Architecture. His research deals with developing methods to discover why we don't know much about the idea of design and finding ways to value why "not-knowing" is an essential beginning point for practice. Bremner is coauthor (with Paul Rodgers) of Design Schools: Beyond Education, Research, Practice and Disciplines (2018).

Paul A. Rodgers is Professor of Design at Imagination, Lancaster University, UK. He holds a Master of Design and a PhD in Product Design Assessment. Rodgers is author or coauthor of nine books including The Routledge Companion to Design Research (2015). His current research interests include hybrid creative practice, experimental design research methodologies, and how disruptive design interventions can enact positive change in health and social care.

+ DESIGN

Anthropocene (an·thro·po·cene), noun

The current geological age, the Anthropocene, is widely viewed as having begun about 200 years ago with the industrial revolution and the consequent impact of human activity on the ecosphere. The World Wildlife Fund's 2010 *Living Planet Report* paints a truly horrendous picture of our current situation that shows our demand on natural resources has doubled since 1966.[1] At the same time, the worldwide economy has grown massively: Gross World Product (GWP) reached 69 trillion dollars in 2008 from only 6.6 trillion dollars in 1950. Thus, in less than 60 years, GWP has increased more than tenfold. This relentless pursuit of financial gain has obvious limits – a truly atrocious ecological crisis. Design in the 21st century faces two massive challenges: the realization of future visions with finite resources and the realignment of a fairer global economic system.

Business (busi·ness), noun

The cultures of design and business are different, although not irreconcilable. Design often celebrates the success of the "star" designer and the importance of creativity. Business, too, values these concepts; but in business, what really matters is profit. Surprisingly, however, the etymology of the word "business" does not equate to capitalism. Business has its roots in the late 14th-century word *bisignes*, referring to "care, anxiety, occupation," and it is the claim to be busy that has perversely become a dominant virtue within capitalism (as well as in design). "Sorry, I'm busy" has become the religious mantra of the worker, but also of the designer and the cultural producer.

Crises (cri·ses), noun

Design (practice, education, research) must acknowledge that it has contributed to the creation of a world that nobody really wants. An ecological crisis wherein we continue to deplete and degrade our natural capital on a massive scale has resulted in one-third of our agricultural land disappearing over the past 40 years, which will inevitably lead to food supply crises and an anticipated doubling of food prices by 2030.[2] A social crisis, which sees nearly 2.5 billion people on our planet living in abject poverty. And a spiritual crisis where, according to World Health Organization statistics, three times as many people die from suicide as die from homicide or in wars.[3] The reality, of course, is that without crises design is a waste of time!

Death (death), noun

"The death of the designer is upon us and has been for some time," proclaimed Adam Richardson in 1993.[4] Fast-forward 25 years and the debates concerning design and its crisis in education, research, ethics, relevance, and value appear to parallel those discussed in Richardson's paper where he asked: "What are the impacts of design's products in societal and cultural contexts, and are these impacts important?" The likes of Victor Papanek and the Italian Counter-Design movements of the 1960s sounded similar warnings, which have since largely been ignored.[5] But news of design's death might be a little premature. Perhaps, as John Thackara suggests, design is in the process of being reborn where designers focus their attention not on objects, buildings, and things but rather acknowledge their role as being key facilitators of social change.[6]

Education (ed·u·cat·ion), noun

In an era where the costs of tuition and students' resulting debts have spiraled out of control, some have questioned whether a design degree

is still worthwhile.[7] While some critics claim that today's designers are poorly trained to meet the demands of the contemporary world, a number of design schools have responded by turning their focus to pressing social, cultural, economic, and environmental issues; working collaboratively and differently across disciplinary, conceptual, methodological, and geographical boundaries and often achieving real impact.

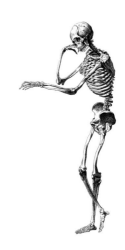

Death

Form (form), noun

The Munich Design Charter of 1990 aimed to animate discussions on the fundamental role to be played by design in the future Europe.[8] The signatories sought a more balanced and ecological model of development for Europe's industrial and social systems that acknowledged that the systems we live in have both physical limits (beyond which lie environmental disaster) and political limits (beyond which lie dysfunctional forms of social coexistence and dictatorship). They believed design was in danger of becoming dedicated to producing strategies of socio-economic legitimation and instead wished to see design's role as one that would put forward new and profound ways of creating a more advanced ecological balance between human beings and the artificial environment they inhabit. Over 25 years later, the Munich Design Charter's relevance is clear as we once again wrestle with huge social, political, and cultural problems while needing to shape new visions for a more peaceful, inclusive, and fairer world.

Global (glob·al), adjective

According to Marshall McLuhan, print gave us the single city and electronic media the global village, and today the crisis of the city is couched in terms of the global city. And just as the global financial platform is the derivative, so too the global city is a derivative so generic that it can only be imported. Rem Koolhaas proposed that the omission of three elements from the history of architecture had insulated us from the fact that all architecture is unwittingly producing a single global junkspace. Similarly, Peter Sloterdijk advanced the idea we are living in a planetary atmosphere that is essentially a global interior that we have already air-conditioned.[9] By contrast to the notion that the advent of digital technologies has created a global city, it appears the digital has no respect for the global or the village: no distinction of night-day, inside-outside, work-leisure, private-public, normal-abnormal. The digital, with its cloud of images and words, is projecting future states while preserving failing conditions in the present. Our willingness to disregard the global village also meant we missed McLuhan's warning: "The global village absolutely ensures maximal disagreement on all points...The tribal-global village is far more divisive—full of fighting—than any nationalism ever was...The village is not the place to find ideal peace and harmony. Exact opposite."[10] The global may have erased the local but even if it had not, as McLuhan predicted, the local is not the answer.

Human (hu·man), noun

In the late 1950s, American industrial designer Henry Dreyfuss introduced the world to "Joe" and "Josephine" in his books *Designing for People* and *The Measure of Man*.[11] Joe and Josephine helped establish human factors and ergonomics as part of the science of design and position humans (or users) at the center of design. Soon their offspring were cast in numerous roles from driving cars to operating spacecraft. Around the time of their inception, Marshall McLuhan proclaimed that objects were invisible and only relationships between objects were visible. If we follow McLuhan's aphoristic logic, Joe and Josephine were never the measure of man. Their conception only ever really illustrated an invisible world – a world in which relationships are made increasingly uncomfortable by design.

Interpassivity (in·ter·pas·siv·i·ty), noun

The world is full of interactive products, services, and experiences. Our fingers endlessly press, swipe, and stretch digital screens and buttons that remind us how busy we are, where the local pizza parlor is, and how many calories we have burned today. But most of these interactions are one-sided. Slavoj Žižek has coined the term "interpassivity" to describe this pseudo-interaction.[12] In Žižek's view, interactive objects largely cannibalize our enjoyment of life and this so-called interactivity is better described as interpassivity. Truly innovative interactive design requires a consequential and

meaningful exchange that stimulates, provokes, or questions its users. If the designed object, space, or experience does not, then it is merely entertainment that exploits magical novelty to achieve false consciousness.[13]

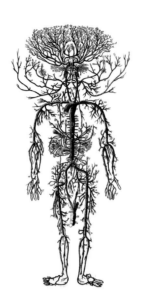

Human

Jealousy (jeal·ou·sy), noun

Jealousy has long been associated with design. An ancient Greek tale tells of a jealous potter so keen to guard his competitive advantage that he never reveals his techniques.[14] This may explain why so little is known of the techniques of the masters of Renaissance and baroque painting – an almost universal secrecy maintained by workshop tradition. But jealousy is not always bad. Among the ancient Greeks, the concept of jealousy was overwhelmingly positive, more closely approximating zeal than jealousy as understood today, while in modern Greek, there is a verb "to make oneself jealous," expressing esteem, admiration, or praise. These conceptions extend to an abstract noun describing a creative act or work of art which is worthy of jealousy, the object of emulation, envy, or ambition. So, perhaps, the measure of good design is the degree of envy it raises in a competitor.

(not) Knowing (know·ing), noun

In 2002, then US Secretary of Defense Donald Rumsfeld made his now-famous statement: "Reports that say that something hasn't happened are always interesting to me because, as we know, there are known knowns; there are things we know we know. We also know there are known unknowns; that is to say, we know there are some things we do not know. But there are

also unknown unknowns – the ones we don't know we don't know." Slavoj Žižek extrapolated from Rumsfeld's three categories a fourth: the unknown known, that which we intentionally refuse to acknowledge that we know.[15] What do these mean for design? First, there are the known knowns where the discipline safeguards the design of imitative objects that consumers find in department stores, and now more frequently online. Second, there are the known unknowns where the discipline knows where it needs to go (e.g., designing a better world) but the perceived millstone of responsibility ensures design will never go there. Third, there are the unknown unknowns where the disciplines have unknowingly coated design with unknowable layers, like sustainability and ethics and responsibility. Last is the unknown known. This is the unassailable modern project (whose product we know is the totally artificial world) plus the prosaic project for the better world (that we know is only better for those who already have everything). But we don't *want* to know that the culture, discipline, and practice of design is engaged in creating inequality, weapons of war, and surveillance networks.

Like (like), verb

"The Becoming Topological of Culture" is an initiative investigating the transformations taking place on the surfaces of society and culture, asking how the digital is deforming and transforming rather than rupturing and disconnecting society and culture.[16] Since the becoming topological culture is driven by social networks deforming public life into "friendships" and commercial networks transforming public space into pay-for-use entertainment, this concerns design because its topos (place) is the interface of these networks. That is, the retreat from the public dimensions of life and space into the artifice of the web has been underwritten by the design of ways to network. These networks have then swept up vast amounts of digital information (mainly images and their tags) into clouds that are seeded by one key button: like. Hitting the like button for someone or something deforms the space-life cloud and new connections rain down creating new topologies of new likes. The identification that humanity has entered a new geological era—the Anthropocene—which is tilting the planet toward a cataclysmic future, is sorely disconnected from like and its thumbs-up icon.

Mongrel (mon·grel), adjective

Design, just like fine art before it, has undergone something of a major transformation in recent years, refocusing its lens to privilege ideas over aesthetics. As such, today, design can be anything. Bruno Latour famously claimed that "design has been expanding ferociously from the design of objects that we use on a daily basis to cities, landscapes, nations, cultures, bodies, genes, political systems, the way we produce food, to the way we travel, build cars, and clone sheep."[17] If you study how design is celebrated nowadays by the likes of the UK's Design Council, you will see that its "winners" range widely from drugs that enhance sexual performance to business software. Stuart MacDonald describes this new creative landscape as a "post-modern soup" in which cultural, economic, social, and educational issues are swimming and where "mongrel" institutions will flourish.[18] But if design can be anything, then it can also be nothing and this perhaps is the biggest challenge that design now faces.

Natural (nat·u·ral), *adjective*

In the Anthropocene, we are reluctantly coming to realize that our artificiality is now our most natural state. In this era of self-production there is no depth to being, only surface or how we appear. This is the terrain of design – what Boris Groys calls the "obligation to self-design" where "design is practiced as a production of differences."[19] Appearance can be redesigned infinitely and this is the perfect scenario for the continuous flow of capital. Having filled up our living spaces with the project of mass-production, the perfect landscape for the protraction of mass-consumption is the body skating across the surface of the mercantile-spectacular. In the project of change (couched as progress in liberal democracies) there used to be a measurable temporal gap between what was changed and new, and what would eventually become natural. But the accelerated culture in which we live means that all change (and by default all artificiality) is now immediately natural. In this hyper-modern condition, design is almost entirely engaged in a project producing indiscernible differences – it is changing the planet.

Oxymoron (ox·y·mo·ron), *noun*

Klaus Krippendorff's 2007 essay "Design Research, an Oxymoron?" argues that research as it is practiced today cannot serve as a model for generating knowledge about design or to improve design.[20] He states that relying on research in its current conservative state will condemn design to mere elaborations of the past. He lists a number of contradictions between what scientific researchers claim they do and what design researchers do such as: science is concerned with what exists, whereas design is concerned with what ought to be; scientific research conserves the status quo, whereas design research breaks with determinisms of the past; and, science celebrates generalizations, abstract theories, and general laws, whereas design suggests courses of action that must ultimately work in the future. But while design research may linguistically be an oxymoron, practically speaking design research is making significant contributions

to numerous global issues all over the world.[21] Design researchers, in collaboration with other disciplinary expertise in business, engineering, computing, and healthcare, update and exploit a variety of conceptual, methodological, technological, and theoretical approaches whilst generating new knowledge about design and many other areas. These projects do not produce mere elaborations of the past, they generate truly creative and transformative interventions that help to shape our lives in more responsible, sustainable, and meaningful ways.

Past

Past (past), *noun*

Perhaps design needs an alternative history. Not a counter-cultural version of a history of design, but another way to present what most designers seek to avoid: the past. Design is enacted in the permanent present, with the seductive allure of the future. The most familiar is the simple past where imitation (not ideas) fuels the project of production and consumption. There is the present perfect where digital flows made it possible to reconnect idea to manufacture turning everyone into prosumers. There is the past perfect, which describes the history of design framed by one investment – faith in technological progress. There is the simple future where the digital production of nothing crafts new producers and ideas are reduced to derivatives. There is the future perfect, still framed by one investment but this time digitally networked progress. And finally, there is the problem of the future in the past, the history/theory of design. Here we get to the core of design's carelessness with its past because design has no choice but to return to its original problem – the contest between being and becoming.

Queer (queer), *verb*

As an adjective, the word queer has a colorful and graphic pattern of use. As a verb, it has been less dynamic: "to queer" has not only meant to

unsettle or upset something or someone but is also used to investigate the foundations of something (in this meaning, to queer is more method than moniker). What does this have to do with design? As both adjective and verb, queer is a good way to describe the Anthropocene, whose impact (fanned by the industrial revolution) is producing a future characterized by both the stagnation of the political imagination and a boom in scientific visualization. The Anthropocene is queer because in geological terms it is upon us and we don't have any real idea of what will result from the profligate burning of finite reserves of fossil fuel. It is producing some pretty queer politics – periodic promises to reduce carbon emissions that every political party at every election seems very willing to break. Meanwhile science has been trying to queer the Anthropocene – to find its future in its origins. It runs into trouble here because in geological terms a methodological track record doesn't exist, turning science into dogma with believers and skeptics. It is at this point that design intelligence (and not intelligent design) might be useful, because from its origins in the industrial revolution it has been making do with method in order to project the possible, and it is futures that we can live in that are needed.

Research (re·search), *noun*

For the majority of design schools throughout the world, research is big business. In many national contexts, a design school's research rankings are vital currency, critical to attracting high-caliber and fee-paying students. Establishing those rankings requires an increased emphasis on research and publication; this may be good business for academics but how does society benefit? This question lies at the heart of many research bodies' criteria for funding, which now routinely look for a high return on investment (RoI) on research projects. Somewhat different from curiosity-driven, exploratory, uncertainty-acknowledging research, some believe this should now be called "RoI-search."[22]

Sustainibility (sus·tain·a·bil·i·ty), *noun*

There is general misconception about which end of the cow produces the methane contributing to global warming. The answer is the front end (cows belch methane), and it appears that this is important to know if you are serious about sustainability. But this seemingly innocuous question is very revealing about the way sustainability is framed. The real "end" we should be questioning is which end of the global animal known as liberal-capitalism produces unsustainability? Clearly, it is the "big end," but the sustainability agenda seems to be aimed at the little end, and this agenda does not appear to have had much impact on the unsustainable practices of the liberal-capital flow of waste fueled by its ability to endlessly invent money in the form of debt. The sustainability agenda demonstrates that consumers can be persuaded to politely burp sustainability, while capitalism belches unsustainability.

Tired (tired), *adjective*

Franco Berardi, aka "Bifo," founder of the renowned Radio Alice in Bologna and an important figure of the Italian Autonomia Movement, points out that tiredness has always been a bugbear to the dream of modernism, the endless thirst for economic growth and profit, and the denial of organic limits.[23] We now have a world that is seriously unprepared to deal with the mounting crises we face because we have based our ways of life on the identification of energy, have an overriding obsession with accumulation, property, and greed, and strive for continual expansion and social well-being. But if we were to contemplate a creative consciousness of tiredness, as Berardi proposes, the current crises may mark the beginning of a massive abandonment of competition, consumerism, and dependence on work and help address the contemporary malaise.

Urban (ur·ban), *adjective*

As the demographers charted the growth of the world's population and capital underwrote its exit from the countryside, a lot of effort and intellect has been focused on the crisis of the urbanizing planet. The result is we probably now know more about the future of the city than its present. However, the migration from rural to urban is leaving the countryside in an intractable position. The path to the Anthropocene began when villages, towns, and cities were shaped from an agricultural landscape. As such, the relationship between the rural landscape and townscape is clearly defined by the historic boundaries between agriculture and urban culture creating rural islands of populations. The population remaining on these rural islands is experiencing massive change driven by a range of factors including climate change and variability, multi-governmental policies, the degradation of arable land, shifts in consumer demand for produce, increased global competition, and technological innovation. Not only is arable land degraded, it is now being consumed by surrounding forests or deserts because no-one cultivates it anymore. The concept of regional development, once imagined to be unlimited, is now on a collision course with new kinds of limits—limits to biodiversity and limits to the flows of energy and water—in contrast to increasingly unlimited digital flows (mostly forms of genetic experimentation and entertainment), leaving rural communities to compete globally for population and productivity.

Virtues (vir·tues), *noun*

Design needs to be more virtuous. In a 1997 lecture, Gui Bonsiepe proposed six virtues for design in the next millennium (lightness, intellectuality, public domain, otherness, visuality, and interest in theory) based on Italo Calvino's *Six Memos for the Next Millennium*.[24] Calvino's definition of "lightness" concerns removing weight from the structure of stories and language, and Bonsiepe finds clear parallels in design, where lightness is a virtue to maintain especially when we reflect on material and energy flows and their environmental impacts. Intellectuality, Bonsiepe's second virtue of design, calls for a more critical stance in design culture. That is, design and writing about design should no longer be seen as sterile and mutually exclusive opposites; rather, intellectuality should reveal contradictions, and compare "what is" to "what could be." The third design virtue is concern for the public domain; that is, we should strive to maintain care for details in everything we do—from address labels to train timetables—that ultimately reflects the kind of society we want to live in. The fourth virtue of design is otherness, or better *concern* for otherness. Today design and design discourse largely reflect the interests of the dominant economies that are engaged in the process of shaping the world according to their hegemonic interests and visions. The virtue of otherness bypasses the weary distinction between developed and underdeveloped nations and instead accepts other design cultures and their values. The fifth virtue is visuality: privileging thinking in terms of images over thinking in terms of texts. Bonsiepe believes the move towards visualization would benefit many, including the way we practice and theorize subjects in the humanities, the physical and biological sciences, and the social sciences. The final virtue of design is interest in theory. Here, Bonsiepe claims that design theory must become part of our future educational programs for two reasons: first, every form of professional practice occurs within a theoretical framework; and second, professional practice that does not produce new knowledge has no future.

Wacky (wa·cky), *adjective*

The industrial revolution transformed the world through truly remarkable manufacturing, technological, and transportation developments. However, some of these can now be seen as plain wacky. We have stripped the earth of natural energy resources and, since the 1960s, have had to produce more and more food to feed a rapidly increasing global population. This has resulted in huge losses of natural habitat, pollution, overfishing, and an unprecedented decline in species throughout the world. Some of the wackier aspects of our current designed predicament include our increasing reliance on water. Water is used to produce everyday items we consume such as meat, cotton, and mobile phones. It takes, for example, around 3,000 liters of water to produce a single hamburger. However, the really wacky fact is that it takes four liters of water to produce a one-liter plastic bottle to hold the water. Water wastefully used to produce bottles to hold water![25]

Xanax (xan·ax), *noun*

Xanax, designed to treat anxiety and panic attacks, is the most popular drug in the United States. In 2009, nearly 50 million prescriptions were written for Xanax and its generic equivalents in the US, representing 20% of all prescriptions. The most contentious effect of the Anthropocene—climate change—opens up the possibility of a new mass anxiety, this time an anxiety for history because the uncertainty of global warming hints at the finitude of humanity. Having discovered planetary limits, we are now facing the possibility we have discovered not just our limits but our end. So too, design finds itself in a new anxiety-producing state, its preferred state once achieved from the pursuit of the question "what-might-become" can now only be "what-might-not-become?"

Yahoos

Yahoo (ya·hoo), *noun*

Before utopia became a genre of satire, Jonathan Swift wrote a satire of utopia – *Gulliver's Travels*. In one episode Gulliver ends up preferring the company of horses to the beasts resembling humans called yahoos. Several centuries later, the story of how the web search engine known as Yahoo came into being seems to also revolve around a part of the world where the epithet "yahoo" is still used to describe company you don't want to keep. The proverb says we are judged by the company we keep, but now that company is creating the coming topological culture – the computational shaping of both voluntary and involuntary networks. By design, it is increasingly difficult to exercise choice over whose company you prefer. A couple of massive beasts of companies already know what and who you prefer and where you are acting out what they know about your preferences. This is not a utopia, nor necessarily a dystopia. As Vilem Flusser pointed out, we have always had designs on each other so machinic life might well be the ideal world for design. If so, the act of design becomes a satire of itself: while claiming rights over the possibilities of what-might-become it gives shape to what-will-not-become, unless Yahoo prefers it.

Zombie (zom·bie), *noun*

In the hunt for meaning for the word innovation and its sidekick creativity, game design is always the case study *par excellence* of governments, design councils, and design schools. As such many design schools have retooled to launch graduates as game designers working from their bedrooms in the hope that their contribution to the design of games, usually at little cost to game magnates, will make them rich and famous. But working for next to nothing within the new wave of the creative industries as the next wave of innovative entrepreneurs of liberal capital is in fact a precarious existence. The whiz-kid dream, based on selling one's skill for very little return, is making design a soulless corpse, which is the very definition of a zombie.

1 World Wildlife Fund, *Living Planet Report 2010: Biodiversity, Biocapacity and Development* (Geneva: WWF International, 2010).

2 Stephen Emmott, *10 Billion* (London: Penguin, 2013).

3 World Health Organization (WHO), *World Report on Violence and Health: Summary*, Geneva: WHO, 2002).

4 Adam Richardson, "The Death of the Designer," *Design Issues* 9, no. 2 (1993): 34–43.

5 Victor Papanek, *Design for the Real World: Human Ecology and Social Change* (London: Thames & Hudson, 1985).

6 John Thackara, *In the Bubble: Designing in a Complex World* (Cambridge: The MIT Press, 2006).

7 A. Davidson, "Is University Still the Answer? Yes, to a Degree...," *Design Council Opinion* (August 14, 2014).

8 Rams, D. et al., "The Munich Design Charter," *Design Issues* 8, no. 1 (1991): 74–77.

9 Philippe Rahm, "Trading Spaces: A Roundtable on Art and Architecture" *Artforum International* (October 1, 2012), 208.

10 Marshall McLuhan in Gerald E. Stearn (ed.), *Hot & Cool: A Primer for the Understanding of and a Critical Symposium with Responses by Marshal McLuhan* (Middlesex: Penguin, 1968), 314–15.

11 Henry Dreyfuss, *Designing for People* (New York: Simon & Schuster, 1955), ch2; Henry Dreyfuss, *The Measure of Man: Human Factors in Design* (New York: Whitney Library of Design, 1960).

12 Slavoj Žižek, *The Plague of Fantasies* (London: Verso, 1997).

13 D. West, "The Work of Art in the Age of Mechanical Interaction," in Paul Rodgers & Michael Smyth (eds), *Digital Blur: Creative Practice at the Boundaries of Architecture, Design and Art* (Oxford: Libri Publishers, 2010), 224–30.

14 R. Nelson, *The Jealousy of Ideas: Research Methods in the Creative Arts* (Australia: Ellikon, 2009).

15 Slavoj Žižek, "What Rumsfeld Doesn't Know That He Knows About Abu Ghraib," *In These Times* (May 21, 2004).

16 Celia Lury, Luciana Parisi & Titziana Terranova, "Introduction: The Becoming Topological of Culture," *Theory, Culture & Society* 29, no. 4/5 (2012): 3–35.

17 Bruno Latour, "A Cautious Prometheus? A Few Steps Towards a Philosophy of Design (With Special Attention to Peter Sloterdijk)," Keynote Lecture for the Networks of Design Meeting of the Design History Society, Falmouth, Cornwall (September 3, 2008).

18 Stuart MacDonald, *Designs on Democracy: Architecture and Design in Scotland Post Devolution* (London: Zero Books, 2012).

19 Boris Groys, "The Obligation to Self-Design," *e-flux Journal* 00 (2008).

20 Klaus Krippendorff, "Design Research, an Oxymoron?" in Ralf Michel (ed.), *Design Research: Essays and Selected Projects* (Zurich: Birkhäuser Verlag, 2007), 67–80.

21 Paul Rodgers & J. Yee, *The Routledge Companion to Design Research* (UK: Routledge, 2015).

22 M. Alvesson, "Do We Have Something to Say? From Research to Roi-search and Back Again," *Organization* 20, no. 1 (2012): 79–90.

23 Franco Berardi, "Exhaustion and Senile Utopia of the Coming European Insurrection," *e-flux Journal* 21 (2010).

24 Gui Bonsiepe, "Some Virtues of Design," based on a lecture given at the "Design Beyond Design" symposium at Jan van Eyck Akademie, Maastricht, The Netherlands (November 1997).

25 Emmott, *10 Billion*.

IMAGE CREDITS

A Report to An Academy

p. 100: Composite image by Alexandra Lillehei, incorporating photograph of Frank Lloyd Wright (1954) by Fay Euine Jones, and photograph of Marion Mahony Griffin (1935), author unknown, courtesy Australian National Library.

Terrarium: The Ultimate Design Experiment

p. 102–103: Image by James Billingsley, used with permission.

p. 105: "The Vivarium" by Henry Noel Humphrys (1810–1879), public domain.

p.106: Montréal Biosphere (May 1976), author unknown, used under CC BY 2.0 license via Wikimedia Commons (altered).

p. 109: (from top): "The garden in Bios-3" © Sputnik/A.Belenogov via sputniknews.com; "Biosphere II in Crisis" © Janette Kim (2008), used with permission; "SpaceGarden" © Orbitec industries.

A is for Anthropocene: An A–Z of Design Ecology

p. 110: Image of old book cover by Ben Hosking (2010), used under CC BY 2.0 license via flickr.com.

p. 111–113: Engravings by A.J. Deefehrt for Encyclopédie by Denis Diderot and Jean le Rond d'Alembert (1751), public domain (altered).

p. 114: "The Servants Drive a Herd of Yahoos into the Field," by Louis John Rhead, public domain (altered).

LA+

Issue 10 of LA+ Journal brings you the results of the **LA+ ICONOCLAST** open design ideas competition, in which we asked designers to reimagine New York's Central Park, fictionally devastated by eco-terrorists protesting the loss of the world's forests. See what designers did when faced with the opportunity to challenge this icon of landscape architecture. LA+ ICONOCLAST also features interviews with jurors Geoff Manaugh (BLDGBLOG), Jenny Osuldsen (Snøhetta), Charles Waldheim (Harvard GSD), Beatrice Galilee (The Met Museum), Lola Sheppard (Lateral Office), and Richard Weller (PennDesign), as well as an essay by *Large Parks* coeditor Julia Czerniak.

OUT FALL 2019

LA+

SIMULATION FALL 2016

LA+

IDENTITY SPRING 2017

LA+

RISK FALL 2017

LA+

IMAGINATION SPRING 2018

LA+

LA+

INTERDISCIPLINARY JOURNAL
OF LANDSCAPE ARCHITECTURE

LA+

TIME FALL 2018

LA+

DESIGN SPRING 2019

LA+

ICONOCLAST FALL 2019

LA+

VITALITY SPRING 2020

LA+ (Landscape Architecture Plus) from the University of Pennsylvania School of Design is the first truly interdisciplinary journal of landscape architecture. Within its pages you will hear not only from designers, but also from historians, artists, philosophers, psychologists, geographers, sociologists, planners, scientists, and others. Our aim is to reveal connections and build collaborations between landscape architecture and other disciplines by exploring each issue's theme from multiple perspectives.

LA+ brings you a rich collection of contemporary thinkers and designers in two issues each year. To subscribe follow the links at WWW.LAPLUSJOURNAL.COM